URBAN REAL ESTATE INVESTMENT
A NEW ERA OF OPPORTUNITY

HENRY CISNEROS • Foreword by Eric Garcetti, Mayor of Los Angeles

Urban Land Institute

About the Urban Land Institute

The mission of the Urban Land Institute is to provide leadership in the responsible use of land and in creating and sustaining thriving communities worldwide. ULI is committed to

▶ Bringing together leaders from across the fields of real estate and land use policy to exchange best practices and serve community needs;

▶ Fostering collaboration within and beyond ULI's membership through mentoring, dialogue, and problem solving;

▶ Exploring issues of urbanization, conservation, regeneration, land use, capital formation, and sustainable development;

▶ Advancing land use policies and design practices that respect the uniqueness of both the built and natural environments;

▶ Sharing knowledge through education, applied research, publishing, and electronic media; and

▶ Sustaining a diverse global network of local practice and advisory efforts that address current and future challenges.

Established in 1936, the Institute today has more than 34,000 members worldwide, representing the entire spectrum of the land use and development disciplines. Professionals represented include developers, builders, property owners, investors, architects, public officials, planners, real estate brokers, appraisers, attorneys, engineers, financiers, academics, students, and librarians.

ULI relies heavily on the experience of its members. It is through member involvement and information resources that ULI has been able to set standards of excellence in development practice. The Institute has long been recognized as one of the world's most respected and widely quoted sources of objective information on urban planning, growth, and development.

About the ULI Center for Capital Markets and Real Estate

The ULI Center for Capital Markets and Real Estate focuses on real estate finance, real estate industry and investment trends, and the relationship between the capital markets and real estate. The mission of the Center is to promote understanding of the real estate capital markets and to provide leadership in fostering a healthy and productive real estate industry and capital markets sector that in turn promote thriving and sustainable communities worldwide. The Center pursues this mission through research, trend analysis, education, events, publications, web-based resources, and thought leadership.

© 2015 by the Urban Land Institute
1025 Thomas Jefferson Street, NW
Suite 500 West
Washington, DC 20007-5201

Cover image: Detroit
Photo credit: Ryan Southern

Library of Congress Cataloging-in-Publication Data

Cisneros, Henry.
 Urban real estate investment : a new era of opportunity / Henry Cisneros.
    pages cm
 Includes bibliographical references and index.
 ISBN 978-0-87420-358-5 (alk. paper)
 1. Real estate investment—United States. 2. Real property—United States. 3. Land use, Urban—United States. 4. Real estate investment—United States—Case studies. I. Urban Land Institute. II. Title.
 HD257.C57 2015
 332.63'240973—dc23
                    2015005407

About the Author

Henry Cisneros is chairman of Cisneros City Group, which invests in urban real estate and infrastructure projects. He is also chairman of CityView, a partner in building and renovating more than 11,000 residential units in 13 states over the last 15 years. Cisneros served four terms as mayor of San Antonio and was secretary of the U.S. Department of Housing and Urban Development in President Bill Clinton's administration. He is currently vice chair of Habitat for Humanity International and chairman of the San Antonio Chamber of Commerce; and in 2007, he was inducted into the National Association of Home Builders' "Builder Hall of Fame." Cisneros holds master's degrees in urban planning and public administration from Texas A&M University and Harvard University, respectively, and a doctorate from George Washington University.

ULI Project Staff

Adrienne Schmitz
Senior Director, Publications
Project Director and Primary Editor

Nicholas Lalla
Analyst
Editor and Contributor

Kathleen B. Carey
Executive Vice President/Chief Content Officer

Dean Schwanke
Senior Vice President, Case Studies and Publications

Anita Kramer
Senior Vice President, ULI Center for Capital Markets and Real Estate

Camille Galdes
Senior Research Associate

James A. Mulligan
Senior Editor

David James Rose
Managing Editor/Manuscript Editor

Betsy Van Buskirk
Creative Director/Graphic Designer

Craig Chapman
Senior Director, Publishing Operations

Contents

Foreword. vi

Acknowledgments viii

Introduction 2

Chapter 1: New Dynamics, New Opportunities. 5

Chapter 2: Prospects for Urban Property Types 11

Chapter 3: Categorizing Cities by
Real Estate Potential 30

Chapter 4: Investment Strategies and Capital Sources. . 47

Chapter 5: 13 Trends behind America's Urban
Paradigm Shift 54

Chapter 6: Case Studies 68

Conclusion 94

Foreword

America's cities are being reborn as new forces to transform the urban environment. Simply put, these are exciting times for metropolitan America. The mid–20th century images of decay that defined U.S. cities are fading away as urban cores throughout the nation are injected with new life.

A new dynamism has emerged through a convergence of new planning principles, renewed civic investment, and an influx of people not forced to move because of a shifting employment landscape, but rather who have made a deliberate choice to repopulate our urban cores.

Los Angeles is well known for its world-class universities, medical facilities, and entertainment companies. Anchor institutions such as the University of Southern California are critical to the new economy of the future.
NSERRANO/WIKIMEDIA COMMONS

Like any change, these forces of renewal come with challenges; we must seek to effect the positive outcomes of regeneration while arresting negative impacts on existing communities.

Henry Cisneros helped lay the foundation for this new life in America's cities. As the young mayor of San Antonio, he helped lead his historic city to reach new heights through sound planning and powerful infrastructure investments. As secretary of the U.S. Department of Housing and Urban Development in the Clinton administration, he visited every state in his work to marshal the transformation of American public housing. Today, as a private sector real estate professional, Cisneros is tackling one of urban America's most pressing issues—how to build for-sale housing for the middle class in our cities. In many ways, the loss of our cities' middle class led to the urban decline of the late 20th century. Our cities must be focused on preventing a repeat of this history.

In this book, my friend captures this important time for our cities. As we come out of the worst recession of our lives, cities are playing a starring role in America's recovery, but urban rebirth does not happen without smart guidance and foundational principles to guide it. From leading the way in new infrastructure investments to bravely tackling the effects of climate change, U.S. cities have reemerged as national centers of political, economic, and social innovation.

But this book is more than a reflection of the moment—it is a playbook for industry and policy makers alike to help guide good policy and smart investments in our urban centers.

This publication comes at a time when the territoriality of the past—"I'm a developer!" and "I'm a resident!" and so on—has steadily, and necessarily, eroded. The silos are breaking down. We are increasingly acting on the interconnectedness of our urban challenges, realizing that traffic congestion is linked with road design and housing affordability or that street-paving programs can incorporate environmental or open-space needs.

In Los Angeles, we have a new Great Streets vision for our neighborhoods that is intended to restore local "main streets" through a holistic approach that incorporates sidewalks, parking, transit, amenities, and business support. At the same time, we are linking local initiatives with our overarching programs—for example, with our regionwide rail program, which is the nation's largest mass transit program. We understand that these rail stations are much more than platforms for train passengers. They are community hubs, economic catalysts, traffic disrupters, and an opportunity for so much more.

The 13 interconnected trends identified in this book give me—the mayor of one of the world's greatest cities—tremendous hope for our future. This guidebook will help accelerate the way in which America's cities are once again becoming the most democratic, livable, and dynamic centers in our country, rooted in the values of opportunity and innovation, and focused on producing the best quality of life for the most people.

The highest room in the Los Angeles City Hall includes an inscription quoting Aristotle: "The city came into being to preserve life; it exists for the good life." In other words, the city was first and foremost a place to find safety and protection, but that is not its final goal. The final goal is to create a place where each one of us can explore what the "good life" means.

In that spirit, I know that this book will inspire us to build American cities that are human-centered, caring, connected, and just. I applaud Henry Cisneros and the contributors for helping those cities become a reality. In my capacity as both a mayor and an urbanite, count me in.

Eric Garcetti
Mayor of Los Angeles

Acknowledgments

The inspiration for this project comes from the continuing work of the Urban Land Institute (ULI) and its chronicling of urban real estate trends. This analysis builds on ULI's annual assessments of urban trends and attempts to extrapolate what they mean for various categories of investment in property types and metropolitan areas over the longer term. Particular appreciation is due to Charles A. Long, whose frameworks for organizing real estate data proved essential. Professor Steven Ott of the University of North Carolina at Charlotte; Jonathan Willer of the Urban Institute; and Mark Weiss, president of Global Urban Development, produced the original studies upon which many of the future projections in this report are based. I appreciate and respect the contributions to this project of ULI's team: Patrick L. Phillips, Kathleen B. Carey, Anita Kramer, Dean Schwanke, Adrienne Schmitz, and Nicholas Lalla. They saw the value of assembling this book and disseminating its message to the national community of city builders. Thanks also go to Brad Case of the National Association of Real Estate Investment Trusts for his assistance.

In addition, I am appreciative of the suggestions and efforts of the initial production team: Carol Ruiz of New Ground; Bill Gloede; Ondine Jarl; and Andrea Sotello of Cisneros City Group.

The hands-on experience with urban projects that has been the principal basis for the ideas in this book comes from my work with the following colleagues: Sean Burton, David Martin, and Victor Miramontes at CityView; Ed Cross at San Antonio Commercial Advisors; Michael Wibracht and Mark Tolley at 210 Developers; and Stefanos Polyzoides of Moules, Polyzoides; and the urban professionals at the city of San Antonio and the U.S. Department of Housing and Urban Development. They have proved their dedication to the planning, financing, and completion of urban projects and their commitment to enhancing cities and urban neighborhoods across the nation. I am grateful to my wife, Mary Alice, who is deeply involved in improving urban life in San Antonio and who provided valuable insights and enthusiastic encouragement throughout this project.

URBAN REAL ESTATE INVESTMENT

A NEW ERA OF OPPORTUNITY

Introduction

The ancient Greek historian Heraclitus shared with posterity a powerful kernel of wisdom: "No man ever steps in the same river twice, for it is not the same river and he is not the same man." He used this syllogism to explain that things change. In his example, the water in a river is constantly moving downstream and past us and as things change, they create new realities. One aspect of human history for which Heraclitus's observation is certainly valid involves the evolution of cities, for which change is constant.

Navigating the Kamo River Rapids in Kyoto, Japan.
© 2008 JEFFREY FRIEDL

We know that many of the basic forces that drive societal change occur in cities. Population, demographics, new forms of conveyance, advances in technology, transitions in economic functions, and alterations of social mores—these forces generate the changes that throughout history have shaped the form, function, and essence of cities.

Heraclitus's wisdom can also be interpreted to mean that human acceptance of change must lead to action in order to be relevant and responsive to new times. Again, his wisdom is applicable to the historical progress of cities. Throughout the ages, cities have responded to the forces of change by recycling older neighborhoods and growing completely new districts, reconfiguring land planning to relate to the next generation of transportation modes, introducing architectural and construction innovations, building the spaces and infrastructure for emergent economic sectors, and integrating social and equity agendas.

This book's challenge is to explore the relationship between the forces of change affecting U.S. cities and the challenges of innovation for the real estate development and real estate finance professions. I believe that identifiable forces are changing America's cities in profound ways, and I believe that many of the most positive forces are converging to create a renaissance in our urban areas. Our cities are the dynamos of a metropolitan nation. Our cities and metropolitan complexes are playing larger roles as global trade centers, their new-economy sectors are replacing legacy industries, their communications and transportation infrastructure is being transformed by technological innovations, their land use decisions are beginning to take into account environmental realities including climate change, and their diversity of population is being linked to the stimulation of urban life and to the opportunities the urban environment presents. We live in a time when these changes are accelerating, and their cumulative effect creates a panoply of opportunities and responsibilities for professionals in urban development and urban real estate finance.

This book is an attempt to extrapolate on the cumulative challenges facing cities and what they mean for specific types of real estate activities and for the financial institutions that supply the necessary capital. Every sector of real estate activity is involved: commercial, office, industrial, residential (both rental and for sale), hospitality, and public infrastructure. The convergence of physical, demographic, and economic forces has a notable impact on each of these real estate property types. It follows that it is worth looking beyond the next several years to anticipate the emerging challenges for planning and developing the urban landscape.

Similarly, it is important to look ahead to how the needs, expectations, and institutional frameworks that govern capital and investment decisions can be matched to new real estate realities on the ground. Understanding the interplay between those real estate realities and the architecture of capital will be of immense importance in bringing projects to completion and in seizing the moment when an urban renaissance is attainable.

As in other times of disruption and reformation, of recycling and renewal, innovators will be rewarded with notable accomplishments, economic remuneration, and lasting legacies. While it is beyond our vision to comprehensively chronicle at any given moment all the converging forces bearing on our cities or to precisely forecast how each can be addressed, thoughtful city builders concentrate on understanding patterns and will know the importance of discerning trends in the disparate facts they see. It is my hope that this book will help stimulate the thinking and conversation that will lead to successful projects, which will produce stronger core cities and which will position the metropolitan engines of the United States to propel the nation's progress.

This book explains America's urban renaissance and establishes a framework to identify, understand, and capitalize on the array of real estate opportunities present in cities across the country. I combine quantitative and qualitative factors to place cities into strong, weak, and mixed categories of development potential. The result of that analysis is an important and inspiring conclusion that goes to the heart of this book and to the heart of my life in public service: every U.S. city, irrespective of its economy, market dynamic, and geography, has unique real estate opportunities and potential for progress.

In order to capitalize on those opportunities and to properly position cities for the future, professionals in urban development and real estate finance must do the following:

▶ Focus on affordability and mixed-income inclusion in response to the need for a range of housing types in cities.

▶ Prepare communities and residential products for evolving demographics—seniors "aging in place," students, and cultural groupings.

▶ Create effective linkages to anchor institutions such as universities, medical centers, governmental offices, and corporate and commercial complexes.

▶ Maximize walkability and mixed-use density in urban projects.

▶ Harness the potency of public transit as a development tool.

▶ Integrate attractive public spaces and amenities into urban development.

▶ Prepare for environmental challenges, incorporating sustainable designs, materials, and water- and energy-conservation technologies.

▶ Create incentives for attracting capital (global, pension, other institutional, real estate investment trust [REIT], and public/private) on a larger scale.

▶ Identify new approaches to public/private partnerships, including innovative capital sources, land uses, and financing.

▶ Incorporate computer technology to build smarter homes and buildings to maximize opportunities for remote work and distance learning.

In six chapters, this book lays out a framework for understanding today's urban real estate opportunities. Chapter 1 offers a big-picture view of urban America and the contours of a new era for real estate. Chapter 2 examines prospects for each major urban property type, demonstrating the diversity of opportunities available in the market today and in the years to come. Chapter 3 analyzes select metropolitan areas as focal points for investment by placing cities into four categories of real estate potential. Chapter 4 discusses investment strategies and capital sources, both of which are critical to real estate development. Chapter 5 explains the 13 trends that are converging to create a paradigm shift in urban America. And chapter 6 provides four case studies—real-world examples of the urban issues analyzed throughout this book—to delve into the data to demonstrate how to make wise, forward-thinking real estate decisions.

CHAPTER 1

New Dynamics, New Opportunities

O beautiful for patriot dream
That sees beyond the years
Thine alabaster cities gleam
Undimmed by human tears!
—"America the Beautiful"

Across the globe, for the first time in history, more people now live in cities than in rural areas. The sheer force of population movement to urban areas is propelling consumer markets, economic growth, public infrastructure expenditures, research and scientific investments, and returns on entrepreneurship and innovation in the world's great metropolitan areas. A new age of prosperous, vibrant cities with increasingly diverse populations is at hand that

Houston has been booming, despite the recession, largely because of its strong energy industry.

will provide a myriad of investment opportunities as metropolitan areas morph into the dominant engines of the world economy.

This global trend is evident in the United States. Great cities such as New York, Boston, and Washington, D.C., which a generation ago were suffering a net outflow of residents, are now destinations of choice for those seeking the opportunities of urban life. The nation's tech centers—among them San Francisco, Austin, and Seattle—are suffering shortages of affordable housing due to an influx of new residents. Real estate is booming in the energy cities, including Houston and Denver.

Still, as Aristotle observed, a great city is not to be confused with a populous one. To his point: in the United States, 65 percent of the population lives just in the 100 largest metropolitan areas—but those great centers produce 75 percent of the nation's gross domestic product (GDP), generate 76 percent of knowledge-economy jobs, and account for 78 percent of all patents and research value.[1] Demographers project that by 2050, the United States will have a population of 439 million[2]—an increase of almost 120 million people from nearly 320 million in 2014, with much of that increase occurring in metropolitan areas.[3]

The positive forces converging to strengthen U.S. cities are identifiable and understandable. First, the new American economy is driven by ascendant industry sectors that are concentrated in urban areas: health care and the life sciences, international trade, business and professional services, tourism and hospitality, international trade, technology development and marketing, and new media. The new economy has been replacing the older, manufacturing-driven industrial base. In retrospect, what was called "the urban crisis" of the 1960s and 1970s was much more than an urban breakdown; it was an American industrial transformation. The deindustrialization of the economy pulled jobs out of cities and moved them to green-grass sites in the exurbs, to rural regions of the United States, and overseas. The cities were left with the physical residue of the older economy—the empty factories and polluted sites—and it has taken them more than 50 years to establish their new economic momentum. It is now clearly accelerating.

Other contributors to the urban momentum are anchor institutions—the building blocks of the new economy—such as great universities, medical centers, corporate headquarters, and cultural complexes. The roles that the University of Southern California plays in supporting Los Angeles or that Marquette University has assumed in sustaining Milwaukee neighborhoods are examples of the convergence of their economic importance and their capacities for community service. Great medical institutions, such as the Johns Hopkins Medical Center in Baltimore, have reinvigorated entire sections of major cities. And cultural complexes, such as the New Jersey Performing Arts Center in Newark, contribute cultural vitality as well as fulfill economic purposes.

Still another force at work in the urban rebirth is the positioning of a new breed of city leaders who are entrepreneurial and business oriented. The best mayors are no longer patronage chiefs or just competent managers of basic services. They lead as orchestrators of public/ private partnerships. An analysis of America's best mayors of the 20th century described Mayor Richard Daley of Chicago as one of the nation's most effective. Through iron-fisted political direction and administrative skill, he built Chicago's reputation as "a city that works." But analysts of cities in this century conclude that his son, Mayor Richard M. Daley, was probably a stronger mayor. While he did not enjoy political dominance in the traditional sense, he interpreted his job as bringing public and private resources together to create the momentum that characterizes modern Chicago.

Daley's successor, Rahm Emanuel (elected in 2011), is following in the footsteps of legendary

mayors and faces new challenges following the Great Recession (2007–2009) to maintain Chicago's strong place in the world economy. The best mayors today understand that their role is akin to that of a traffic cop, ensuring that resources and institutions are moving in productive directions and avoiding collisions of public and private interests.

A number of urban dynamics converge to create this era of possibilities for cities. In the most progressive metropolitan areas, community development groups that during the 1960s viewed themselves as adversaries of local government today cooperate with municipal officials as sophisticated developers of neighborhood shopping districts and of workforce housing in redevelopment areas. Empty nesters who want the stimulation of urban life have spurred growth in urban neighborhoods such as Lower Downtown Denver and Deep Ellum in Dallas. Central Atlanta has gained population after 50 years—five

Mayor Richard M. Daly led the development of Chicago's signature Millennium Park, which is known for its cutting-edge architecture, gardens, and sculptural work such as *The Bean*.
CITY OF CHICAGO, MILLENNIUM PARK INC.

census counts—of decline and is now on the upswing because the "creative class" wants to live and work in a vibrant urban setting.

Among larger societal trends strengthening cities are increasing suburban traffic congestion and intensifying environmental concerns, which make workers conscious of the need to be closer to central employment centers and avoid the long commutes that result from suburban sprawl. The smart growth movement emphasizes the efficiencies of modernized infrastructure, such as mass transit. Charlotte, North Carolina, is reaping the benefits of extending a light-rail line from its central business district to residential neighborhoods, which are now connected to its downtown banking headquarters as never before.

When Hurricane Katrina hit New Orleans in 2005, the city's levees were breached, causing catastrophic flooding. In all, the storm killed more than 1,800 people and caused $108 billion in damage, and serves as a cautionary tale for cities that do not prioritize resilience in urban design. WIKIMEDIA COMMONS

As dynamic engines of economic growth in the new economy, cities will lead the charge toward new and better "green" construction and development. Experts on global sustainability believe that cities must be the focal points of investment to solve the environmental challenges of our time. In a report titled *Reinventing the City*, the World Wide Fund for Nature concludes that, on their present course, cities will generate fully half the total emissions allowable to maintain a livable climate over the next 90 years within just the next 30 years. Put another way, the urban built environment without climate control interventions will generate one-half the total emissions in one-third the allowable time.[4]

While most assessments of climate change focus only on the environmental damage, some business leaders are calculating the economic costs. Resilience—understood to mean a city's ability to prepare for and recover from extreme weather events—has a clear economic component. A study titled *Risky Business: The Economic Cost of Climate Change in the United States*, led by former New York Mayor Michael Bloomberg and former U.S. Secretary of the Treasury Hank Paulson, is designed to calculate such urban real estate impacts as higher flood insurance rates, increased water costs, lower construction productivity, and heightened fire risks.[5]

Recognizing that urban areas worldwide will spend about $350 trillion on the construction, operation, and maintenance of urban infrastructure over the course of those 30 years, cities can lead the way in changing the trajectory of environmental damage. Those infrastructure investments can be environmentally positive and financially sound. The juxtaposition of the scale of that forthcoming urban investment and the urgency of the global environmental problem requires that cities around the world be incentivized to plan advanced infrastructure that promotes environmental sustainability. Cities will lead in deploying new sustainability policies, new urban planning, new infrastructure, new communities, new homes, new building materials, new technologies, and new financing. As hurricanes Katrina and Sandy have painfully demonstrated, the stakes for not addressing climate change impacts and investing in resilience are too high.

These forces and others have created a metropolitan momentum that is both statistically measurable and anecdotally visible. New York City's population reached 8.2 million in the 2010 U.S. Census; that city's planning department is projecting 9 million people by 2040.[6] Nearly a million additional people will need to be housed, go to work, and use transportation systems in New York City. That growth will be the fuel for new developments in the boroughs of Brooklyn, Queens, and the Bronx.

Similar trends are occurring—though on a smaller scale—in America's other global gateway cities: San Francisco, Boston, Miami, Los Angeles, Seattle, Chicago, and Washington, D.C. These trends extend to the new "urban experience cities," places where young talent is attracted to the jobs and lifestyle nexus, such as Dallas, Charlotte, Atlanta, northern Virginia, San Diego, Denver, San Antonio, Houston, and Portland. Urban creative centers affiliated with universities create magnets with their own attraction, as in Austin (the flagship campus of the University of Texas), the Research Triangle (Duke University and the University of North Carolina), Columbus (Ohio State University), and San Jose and the Silicon Valley (Stanford University). Research conducted by the Washington, D.C.–based International Downtown Association concludes: "The nation's urban centers are growing rapidly in

Thin Flats in Philadelphia is an urban apartment building that uses sustainable design. The building's green roof provides an oasis for residents to relax and enjoy the outdoors, all within an urban environment. ONION FLATS LLC

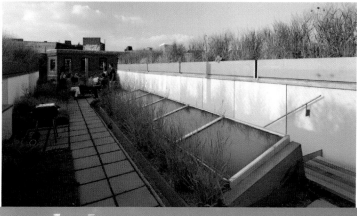

9

population and are now competing equally with suburbs as preferred places to work and live. . . . For decades, cities have been in a process of decline, but cities are rebounding as places to work, as thriving places to shop, and as vibrant places to live."[7]

This metropolitan renaissance will drive a major part of the new construction needed to modernize and expand the nation's built environment. By 2030, the United States will need 426 billion square feet of built environment to provide industrial space and retail and commercial sites—171 billion square feet more than currently exists. In addition, about 60 million square feet of present stock will become obsolete and need to be replaced, resulting in a total of more than 230 billion square feet of space that will need to be built. The growth of population and construction will also be evident in the residential sector. By 2050, the U.S. population is expected to grow from 320 million to 439 million. When projected occupancy patterns are considered, estimates are that growth will generate a need for more than 52 million new housing units, the majority in urban environments.[8]

This growth represents jobs, construction technologies, and investment that will be focused in the United States. It cannot be exported or constructed off shore because it is literally on the ground. In that sense, it is the classic high-priority, domestic industry—and it is indefinite in its duration. There is no end to real estate investment opportunity in cities. When an urban industrial function becomes obsolete—for example, when an old warehouse district is no longer functional because industries have modernized the way they manage logistics—cities can demolish the unsalvageable use and clear the ground to make way for a new structure for the next urban economy. Or the structure can be adapted to more suitable uses for today. This process is underway in city after city across the country: old factory spaces are converted into lofts, Class B office buildings are demolished to make way for modern medical towers, truck yards are transformed into high-tech clean rooms, and warehouse zones are giving way to arts districts and retail amenities.

All of these trends are converging to create a dominant place for cities and metropolitan areas in America's social and economic development and to create unprecedented opportunities for urban real estate professionals. Investing in and building the homes, stores, apartments, offices, hotels, industries, and infrastructure that the U.S. urban renaissance requires will create jobs, launch firms, and require the talents of the world's best real estate, design, construction, and financial professionals.

CHAPTER 2

Prospects for Urban Property Types

While all property sectors were affected by the real estate downturn and the global economic recession that began in 2007, the postrecession opportunities in urban real estate are becoming clear. This chapter describes opportunities for the principal urban property sectors going forward: retail, office, industrial, hotel, infrastructure, for-sale residential, and multifamily rental. It relies heavily on the work of PwC and the Urban Land Institute as presented in their annual publication, *Emerging Trends in Real Estate®*.

The DCUSA retail development in the Columbia Heights neighborhood in northwest Washington, D.C., offers walkable access to big-box retailers like Target and Best Buy.
WIKIMEDIA COMMONS, GRIDPROP

Table 1 categorizes the major property sectors and their principal component types.

Urban Retail

A somewhat nostalgic and increasingly anachronistic image of a thriving retail sector in U.S. cities is that of massive department stores in central business districts, such as Macy's in Manhattan, Nordstrom in Seattle, Neiman Marcus in downtown Dallas, and Marshall Field's in Chicago. While big department stores can be important anchors in the downtowns of cities, the trends of recent decades brought the closing of many traditional department stores. Some changed their roles as they consolidated with other retail chains offering different price points and fashion lines. For example, Marshall Field's—the upscale department store founded in Chicago in 1852, later to become a regional chain—was acquired by Macy's in 2006. The store had deep Chicago roots, and the company's flagship store occupied the iconic Daniel Burnham–designed Marshall Field and Company Building in the downtown Loop. Chicagoans and tourists alike considered the store "as Chicago as it gets," and when Macy's purchased the company and renamed both the building and the store, it sparked a series of organized protests.

Since the mid-20th century, many of the dominant functions of downtown department stores have migrated to suburban fortress malls, frequently located at major freeway interchanges or at other regionally prominent locations easily accessible to suburban shoppers. In recent years, downtown advocates have worked hard to replicate the amenities and conveniences of suburban shopping centers in downtown settings, such as Atlantic Terminal in Brooklyn, Southside Works in Pittsburgh, and Westfield San Francisco Center in San Francisco's South of Market district.

Municipal leaders have recognized that the nature of retailing in cities has changed and requires new real estate configurations. Big-box stores—such as Target, Costco, and Walmart—have become the anchors for urban nodes, built on key arterial streets surrounded by dense catchment zones of consumers in nearby neighborhoods. Also important are neighborhood centers, which host such local services as convenience stores, fast-food restaurants, grooming suppliers, hair and nail salons, repair shops, and laundry services. Retail centers anchored around

TABLE 1: REAL ESTATE PRODUCT TYPES

Retail	Office	Industrial facilities	Hotels/ motels	Infrastructure	For-sale residential	Multifamily rentals
Traditional downtowns	CBD; Class A, B, C	Warehouse/ distribution	Luxury	Transportation	Single-family detached	Luxury
Neighborhood centers	Neighborhood service	Research/ development	Full-service	Communications	Single-family attached	Urban/suburban garden
Power centers	Suburban; Class A, B, C	Manufacturing	Business center	Energy	Multifamily condominiums	Urban high rise
Regional malls	Medical	Data centers	Family travel	Social facilities	Master-planned communities	Student housing
Mixed-use properties	Research and development	Self-storage facilities	Resort	Utilities		Seniors' housing
Lifestyle/ entertainment	Government					Military housing; government-subsidized

Note: Categories defined by Marc Weiss, Global Urban Development.

major grocery stores are mainstays of the urban retail inventory.

Another variation of retail in urban areas is the subregional shopping area, which may include stores specializing in clothing, personal accessories, and upper-end boutique lines. Some such shopping districts serve upscale neighborhoods and consist of chic stores with higher-priced offerings. Examples include Highland Park in Dallas; the Stanford Shopping Center in Palo Alto, California; and upper Wisconsin Avenue in Chevy Chase, Maryland, and Washington, D.C.

Retail in urban areas assumes many forms and drives a substantial segment of real estate economics within cities while contributing

BRINGING BACK BUCKHEAD

Just north of downtown Atlanta, Buckhead Village had long been a nightlife destination for the city's young and hip residents. In recent years, however, the area entered a period of decline that culminated in several violent incidents in and around the area's clubs. Developer Ben Carter Properties began buying up increasingly shabby properties and eventually assembled an eight-acre, six-block parcel at the intersection of Peachtree Road and East Paces Ferry Road, a main thoroughfare into the city. It was to become "Streets of Atlanta," a high-end, mixed-use project that promised retail, restaurant, office, residential, and hotel facilities. Key elements of the plan were walkability and sustainability.

Buckhead Atlanta is a walkable, mixed-use development complete with high-end boutiques, restaurants, and residences. OLIVERMCMILLAN

Then the Great Recession hit. Work was halted in 2008, restarted in 2009, and then stopped again in 2010. The parcel was acquired by San Diego–based OliverMcMillan in 2011, which in turn scaled back the original project to—as the company put it—a "more human scale" in order to appeal to a wider mix of the region's residents. Still maintaining a sense of luxury, the development was renamed "Buckhead Atlanta."

Construction of the project's first phase was completed in January 2014, with occupancy beginning later in the year. The completed 1.5 million-square-foot district will include 800,000 square feet of "customizable space," including 300,000 square feet of upscale retail, 100,000 square feet of office space, and two 12-story buildings containing 370 luxury residences. There also will be 160,000 square feet of retail space with the likes of Hermès, Canali, and Etro boutiques, and 70,000 square feet of space for dining establishments—all served by 2,400 parking spaces.

Buckhead Atlanta's first retail and restaurant tenants opened in fall 2014, and additional tenants will be announced into early 2015. Spanx, the hosiery company, moved into its new Buckhead Atlanta headquarters in 2014. OliverMcMillan hopes that Buckhead Atlanta will revitalize the existing Buckhead Village and raise walkability standards for the Atlanta metropolitian region.

significantly to urban residents' quality of life. Retail in general, however, faces challenges. Recent years have seen a large number of marginal stores close—particularly Class B and Class C properties—and big store failures. The U.S. retail sector shed a million jobs between December 2007 and June 2009.[9] Retail footage per-capita ratios in the United States had become the highest in the world, as much as one-third more than in most other advanced nations. U.S. retail had been overbuilt and as a result vacancy rates will decline ever so slowly over the next few years.[10]

In terms of new developments, very few enclosed malls have been built since 2006. Traditional large-scale malls are confronting massive reinvention as some experts—although not all—have predicted the extinction of the dominant supermall model over the next decades.[11] Retailers and their real estate partners are challenged as online retailing continues to reduce the need for physical store space. As a result, retailers seek smaller spaces and fewer locations. An RREEF Property Trust study found that online purchases account for 5 percent of sales overall, although online purchases claim significantly greater shares of retail transactions for electronics, books, music, and apparel.[12]

However, among the positive signs in the retail sector is the location of high-quality stores in newly strong city neighborhoods, such as the Buckhead area in Atlanta and the Pearl District in Portland. Urban retail is taking the form of infill power centers offering mixed uses, entertainment venues, and ethnic-themed districts. Subregional centers in ethnic neighborhoods anchored by grocery stores have proved to be attractive properties in cities such as Houston and Los Angeles. More attention is being given to transportation-linked urban centers that are less dependent on automobile traffic. Busy young professionals seek convenience and a diversity of walkable amenities. As new urbanist and smart growth concepts continue to gain traction, and as both young and aging urban populations want to drive less, more retail projects will be built as mixed-use projects with residential components and will focus on infill locations with vibrant streets. As more cities encourage the formation of amenity-rich neighborhoods for young professionals, same-sex couples, and empty nesters, upper-end retail stores will gravitate to revived urban business districts such as the Montrose area in Houston.

Office Space

Offices in America's urban settings take many forms, but in most metropolitan areas the traditional central business district (CBD) is the locus of the largest volumes of office square footage. In the CBD, Class B office buildings from the 1950s share the skyline with the most modern Class A trophy towers. Differences in energy efficiency, floor plans, parking arrangements, finishes, and amenities distinguish buildings of different classes. Their differentiated lease rates accommodate a variety of firms and institutions that need to be in the downtown area, which in most cities continues to be the center of government and professional activity.

While many CBDs have experienced the loss of corporate headquarters to suburban office campuses, some firms still need to be near local government offices and courts, as well as law firms and accounting services. New-economy businesses such as software, marketing, business services, trade, financial, and media firms benefit from the urban dynamic, which economists refer to as "agglomeration effects"—namely, the benefits that accrue from proximity to other firms, including expediting transactions, sharing ideas, and deepening social interactions. While Silicon Valley is home to a concentration of established technology companies and venture capital firms, smaller companies and startups, with leaner budgets, are seeking out relatively affordable office space in places such as Austin, Denver, and Boston's tech corridor.

In the first half of the last century, a dominant urban pattern was established in which office density decreased as distance between offices and the CBD increased. The declining scale and volume of office space in the concentric circles outside the CBD were accommodated in low-rise office parks, and in one- or two-story buildings on arterial streets adjacent to residential areas. Professionals providing neighborhood-oriented services such as doctors, dentists, insurance agents, and real estate agents typically occupy such smaller office structures.

Amazon's location in downtown Seattle is a unique example of an urban corporate headquarters. Its dense, walkable design provides workers with direct access to transit, cafés, restaurants, and other downtown amenities.
MICHAEL WALMSLEY

Over the last half-century, however, major office centers have leapfrogged those concentric circles of development to create anchor office nodes in "edge cities" such as Los Colinas in Dallas, Tysons Corner in northern Virginia, and Schaumburg, Illinois—some 30 miles north of Chicago—which often rival the CBD in office and retail square footage. Simply defined, edge cities are concentrations of commercial, retail, and entertainment uses located away from the CBD of a metropolitan area.

During that time, many Fortune 500 companies established massive corporate campuses to consolidate headquarter functions at suburban sites, such as Allstate Insurance Company in Northbrook, Illinois, outside Chicago; PepsiCo in Purchase, New York, outside New York City; and the Facebook and Google campuses in Silicon Valley. Amazon, however, offers a counter example to the edge city, as its Seattle headquarters recently expanded its already substantial downtown presence by adding another half-million square feet in four downtown buildings.

During the Great Recession, landlords reduced rents and provided free improvements as tenants downsized or shopped for better terms elsewhere. Such concessions reduced the profitability of many buildings and locations. Office space is highly dependent on job growth; so when firms cut back employment, they reduced the space they leased, thus weakening the mar-

CLINICAL LIFELINE

In early 2012, the Cleveland Clinic— one of the nation's premiere medical research facilities and Ohio's second-largest employer[13]—unveiled a master plan for its 160-acre main campus, a decidedly urban collection of buildings with a dense core surrounded by deteriorating neighborhoods. The plan centers along a three-quarter-mile "green spine," described by the Cleveland *Plain Dealer* as a nearly continuous corridor of leafy outdoor plazas and inspired by the National Mall in Washington, D.C.

Prepared with the help of Foster + Partners of London, the master plan calls for the construction of 14 new, six-story sustainable buildings arrayed along the spine with existing structures, modified to allow for sight lines and access to the greenway. The master plan provides a blueprint for harnessing Cleveland's dramatic growth as a medical center to spur revitalization of its neighborhoods.

Announced in June 2013, Case Western Reserve University and the Cleveland Clinic will partner to own and operate the university's medical education facility, located on the clinic's main campus.[14] The project was originally planned as a 165,000-square-foot building, but plans have been expanded and now a 485,000-square-foot complex is being planned.[15]

The growth of the Cleveland Clinic's downtown campus has been aided by the $200 million, 6.8-mile Euclid Corridor Transportation Project, dubbed the HealthLine, which opened in 2008. Euclid Avenue connects the central business district with University Circle—a hub of medical facilities that includes the Cleveland Clinic and the University Hospitals of Cleveland; the two institutions purchased the naming rights of the bus rapid transit (BRT) line. This BRT center won a 2011 ULI Award for Excellence and today connects thousands of commuters to their places of work. Although it is premature to identify the master plan's impact in the surrounding area, the Cleveland Clinic is taking promising actions to build a robust campus with the prospect of catalytic impacts throughout downtown.

The Cleveland HealthLine bus rapid transit service links the Cleveland Clinic to the city's other business districts.
SASAKI ASSOCIATES

ket for major new office developments. Because suburban markets were the hardest hit in the economic downturn, many premier developers focused on downtown or near-downtown centers. Overall, the U.S. office market gained strength in 2014, registering quarterly increases in leasing activity.[16] The office vacancy rate for the second quarter of 2010 was 16.8 percent, compared with 14.5 percent at the same time in 2014.[17] In today's economy, the best and most modern office buildings in the business districts of the nation's major cities are highly valued properties and garner the attention of global investors.

A type of office property that seems to be a particularly bright spot for the decades ahead is medical office space, which tends to be concentrated around major urban and suburban hospital complexes. With increases in the needs of the aging baby-boomer population for health care, medical facilities are projected to be in strong demand going forward. Technological advances have made more outpatient services possible, increasing demand for nonhospital facilities. Given the growth of university-based medical research and education, office demand for medical-related firms and services is expected to increase in cities, as has occurred near the Cleveland Clinic, in the area around the University of California, San Diego, and in the Medical Center area in Houston.

The emergence of new leading sectors of the U.S. economy, such as new-media technologies and the workplace culture they foster, require new configurations of office space. For example, the continuing growth of knowledge companies in Silicon Valley is driving a fresh round of office construction that must incorporate new designs for interior workspaces, such as smaller individual offices, readily available workspaces for impromptu teams, and paperless operations; nontraditional amenities, including snack bars, nap spaces, and laundry service; and specialized electrical power infrastructure.[18] It is clear that

technology firms will be major drivers of demand for office space, as software, data storage, and mobile apps firms have made San Francisco the best-performing office market in the United States.

For-Sale Residential

The predominant form of residential unit in most U.S. cities is the detached single-family home. The detached homes in many core urban areas include the large-scale residences built during the last century as industrial barons created neighborhoods in the most desirable settings of cities such as Detroit, Cleveland, Philadelphia, and New York. Early in their histories, some of America's older cities established patterns of attached townhouses, such as the five-story mansions on the upper east side of New York and rowhouses for working families in Philadelphia. In some of these places, those old mansions have badly deteriorated and been torn down.

But the dominant pattern of detached homes in cities is visible in the many square miles of bungalows with various architectural and design themes, as in Chicago, Kansas City, and Los Angeles. During the 1920s and 1930s, the growth of detached single-family homes in neighborhoods created multiple concentric circles spreading from downtown districts. During the 1940s and 1950s, the outward movement resulted in the establishment of the first ring of inner suburbs, such as Evanston, Illinois, adjacent to Chicago and home to Northwestern University; Bethesda, Maryland, on the northwestern edge of Washington, D.C.; and Dearborn, Michigan, next to Detroit. After World War II, as demand for housing for returning soldiers and for the burgeoning middle class exploded, new forms of suburban housing were constructed in communities such as Palmdale, located 50 miles north of Los Angeles, and the Levittowns of Long Island, New York, and Bucks County, Pennsylvania. These eventually led to the modern suburban master-planned community such as the Woodlands, north of

Houston, and the many ranches-turned-suburbs of Orange County, California.

Municipal leaders recognize the importance of continuing to add to their housing stock and acknowledge that cities must have a mix of for-sale housing types, including homes that are affordable to working people as well as higher-priced homes. Because of the high value of land there, affordable and workforce housing in the city core often takes the form of attached housing, such as townhomes, three-story multifamily structures, or adaptations of existing multistory buildings. As cities focus on affordability, the guideline most frequently used is

THE LIFE-SPAN HOME

Today, about 40 million Americans are older than 65 years of age; by 2040, there will be roughly a doubling of the over-65 population to 80 million. Over the same period, the population of 6 million Americans currently over 85 years of age will triple, to about 20 million. The acceleration of the aging of the nation's population is fueled by aging of the baby boomers (i.e., those born between 1946 and 1964). In 2011, the first of the baby boomers turned 65.[19] It is common to think of housing for an aging population as assisted-living facilities or nursing homes. In fact, only about 9 percent of older Americans live in such facilities at any point in time while 91 percent live in conventional housing units alone or with others. More than 90 percent of elderly survey respondents say they want to live independently in conventional houses as long as they can.[20] The challenge for the nation will be to expand the stock of age-appropriate housing for seniors by developing smaller-scale, affordable, for-sale homes and rental units as well as remodeling many existing homes to eliminate barriers and create safer "life-span" environments.

New Millennial Homes of Tampa, Florida, recently received the AARP/National Association of Home Builders Livable Communities Award for its Freedom Home prototype, suitable for both aging and disabled persons. Keith Collins of Millennial Homes states: "We have worked to make our homes barrier-free, universal in design, adaptable, affordable, and multigenerational. . . . We began

The Freedom Home was originally designed for injured veterans, but is also well suited to senior citizens.
NEW MILLENNIAL HOMES

with the very simple concept that people need to be able to maneuver throughout their homes without barriers, limitations, or obstacles. The essential for us began with the concept of visitability—a zero-step entry, bathrooms on the ground floor, and 32-inch entry doors."

Homes range from the 952-square-foot model with two bedrooms and two bathrooms to a 3,200-square-foot model with four bedrooms and three bathrooms. The most popular models sell for about $50 per square foot net of land costs. Age- and disability-related accessorizing is planned into the design in order to reduce costs, to fit creatively into the home, and to avoid conveying an institutional image.

that housing is affordable if a family does not pay more than 30 percent of their gross income for all housing expenses. Workforce housing is generally defined as that which is within the reach of a family earning 60 to 120 percent of the area median income (AMI) and is generally market financed and not eligible for either federal or local subsidies. Increasingly, developers and local governments are cooperating to build mixed-income communities; that is, they incorporate higher-priced units with workforce and affordable housing, in exchange for expedited approvals, reduced permitting fees, and density bonuses.

The for-sale residential sector lay at the heart of the nation's economic crisis of 2007–2009. In the years since then, this sector has functioned at lower levels than it did during its 2005–2006 peak. That was principally attributable to the nation's slow-growing job markets, which undermined buyers' confidence about being able to make home purchase decisions (and their actual ability to purchase). There also are policy issues, such as uncertainty about the roles of the government-sponsored enterprises—Fannie Mae and Freddie Mae—and the prospect of higher interest rates as the Federal Reserve Bank ends the expansive monetary regimen that was used to stimulate the economy. As interest rates rise, mortgage spreads widen and constrain homebuying. Also as a result of the economic crisis, banks now require purchasers to invest more equity and to demonstrate stronger credit histories. The result is a combination of factors that have mitigated against a stronger recovery in the for-sale housing sector. While some areas of the country have rebounded strongly since the Great Recession, other parts have not. A 2013 RealtyTrac report shows a robust recovery in Rochester, New York; Fort Myers, Florida; and Birmingham, Alabama; meanwhile, Baltimore, Philadelphia, and Colorado Springs, Colorado, continue to struggle as does the industrial Midwest.[21] But at the same time, in desirable

East Coast and West Coast areas, the "mansionization" of inner suburbs has continued at a relentless pace—which both lowers the number of affordable houses and gobbles up land that can be used for the development of affordable housing.

However, against the backdrop of those realities are the ongoing deleveraging among consumers as well as projections of U.S. population growth. The United States will undoubtedly rebuild a strong housing sector, but it may take different forms than it has in the past. Some experts expect slower rates of suburban building, juxtaposed with the development of more urban-oriented infill homes at smaller scales and greater densities. But it is premature to describe those projections as indicative of the end of sprawl, because as demand for housing eventually returns to high, or higher, levels, large-scale production must be accommodated where large numbers of lots are available.

Where will the 129 million more people demographers predict by 2050 live?[22] Suburban growth will continue to be important as large production builders work to meet that demand. However, it is likely that the ratio of suburban to urban development will change. While housing development over the postwar years has been predominantly suburban, the U.S. housing sector is entering a period during which the suburban/urban housing mix will likely be more even. Intown employment generators, improved mass transit, smart growth policies, and the costs of commuting will propel momentum toward more urban residential projects. Densifying and urbanizing currently suburban locales represent another facet of urbanization, already well underway in many places, especially where land costs are high.

Homebuilders and urban developers will offer new prototypes of urban residences, including designs with smaller square footage incorporating age-appropriate amenities for the surging senior population. Attention to health considerations will improve housing quality through the use of nontoxic materials, ventilation systems, and energy practices. Housing quality recommendations were outlined in the 2014 report of the National Center for Healthy Housing and the American Public Health Association.[23]

Economists predict that for the first time since 2008, the housing sector will contribute to national gross domestic product (GDP) growth at more normal levels. The wind behind the sails in the housing sector includes low inflation, lower energy prices, state and local government hiring, and the resolution of partisan disputes over the U.S. debt ceiling. Despite the tapering of Federal Reserve efforts to keep interest rates low, economists estimate new-home starts to exceed 1 million units in 2014, existing-home sales to rise, and home prices to strengthen. Housing starts first dipped below 1 million in 2008 and were projected to rise back to 1 million in 2013, but fell short.[24]

In the aftermath of the Great Recession, much discussion has occurred about whether higher levels of homeownership were the cause of the economic crisis. While the postmortems make it clear that many factors caused the housing meltdown—an extended period of low interest rates after the dot-com bust, irresponsible mortgage lending, Wall Street securitization practices, careless rating regimes, and lax governmental oversight—it is likely that national policies will encourage more balance in the approach to homeownership and rental. A substantial portion of the population will always be better suited to renting, including young people who have not yet amassed the savings

SouthSide Works is a mixed-use redevelopment of a former brownfield site on Pittsburgh's South Side. The 123-acre site along the Monongahela River was formerly home to the LTV Steel finishing mill, but now features a riverfront plaza filled with retail uses, offices, restaurants, and residential space.
PIOTRUS/WIKIMEDIA COMMONS

for a downpayment, immigrants who may take as long as a generation before they can become homeowners, and other low-wage workers. There also are renters by choice, who for a range of reasons do not want to be homeowners.

Yet homeownership will continue to be important in the United States. In fact, several studies have shown that the principal vehicles for building the middle class since World War II were three sets of public policies: access to

SILICON POWER

The area around Palo Alto, California, was not always known as Silicon Valley, but it has been a tech center since the middle of the last century, powered by the presence of Stanford University, and has become a global powerhouse in recent decades. Although it lacks the density of traditional urban centers on the East Coast, Silicon Valley is a metropolitan region and considered urban by West Coast standards. Such places are often considered "edge cities," with suburban bedroom communities but also with significant business growth. For Silicon Valley, the growth in business is due to its long history with technology.

Hewlett-Packard (HP) was founded in a rented garage in Palo Alto in 1939. Between 1955 and 1985, research at Stanford funded by companies such as AT&T's Bell Laboratories led to the development of the silicon-based integrated circuit, microprocessors, and microcomputers. During the early 1970s, the Xerox Corporation pioneered the Alto project at its Palo Alto Research Center, which created the world's first graphical user computer interface, which later inspired the founders of Apple Computer to create the Macintosh operating system and Microsoft to develop Windows.

New companies thrived and attracted suppliers, employees, and venture capital firms, which in turn helped create more companies. Several of the biggest names in technology are headquartered in the valley, including Google's "Googleplex" in Mountain View, Apple's headquarters in Cupertino, Intel in Santa Clara, Facebook in Menlo Park, Yahoo in Sunnyvale, HP and Cisco in Palo Alto, and eBay in Campbell. As congestion on the region's two major highways (Interstate 280 and U.S. Route 101) has increased, the area known as the valley has spread northward to San Francisco and Oakland. The animation studio Pixar chose to build its headquarters adjacent to Oakland in Emeryville.

Silicon Valley is a model for generating tech industries, fostering entrepreneurship, and building partnerships between the private sector and research universities. Its global stature and economic output inspired Mayor Michael Bloomberg to develop a burgeoning, small-scale tech center in New York City through a new Cornell University and Technion-Israel Institute of Technology tech campus on Roosevelt Island, just east of Manhattan. Through graduate programs in computer science, media, and business, Cornell's new campus will help students and entrepreneurs partner with local tech companies and develop a tech industry in New York.

The new Cornell Tech campus is modeled after Silicon Valley and will serve as a center for research and technological innovation in New York City. HANDEL ARCHITECTS

higher education, policies for raising incomes and wages, and homeownership. Homeownership is fundamental to sustaining a durable middle class. Given the growth of minority populations and the need to create the next American middle class from a diverse new population, the drive toward homeownership will continue, albeit in a more balanced and responsible fashion, and will be a contributor to growth and stability in America's metropolitan for-sale markets. Government policies, particularly the reform of the government-sponsored enterprises—Fannie Mae and Freddie Mac—to attract more private capital to the housing sector will be needed to help stabilize homeownership for the long run.

Urban Industrial Facilities

As recently as the 1950s, manufacturing was the largest source of jobs and employment in most U.S. cities. A large number of them—especially Rust Belt cities such as Buffalo, Cleveland, Detroit, and Milwaukee—had manufacturing sectors that accounted for up to 30 percent of their total employment bases. Smaller cities such as Akron and Toledo in Ohio, Harrisburg in Pennsylvania, and Rochester in New York also had high percentages of their jobs based in manufacturing.[25] Even cities in the Southwest that were not thought of as manufacturing centers, such as Los Angeles and Dallas, had substantial portions of their economies in manufacturing.

Because manufacturing was the driving engine of the American economy, it was logical that manufacturing clusters would generate the need for housing and for retail businesses and thereby shape America's cities. Massive industrial complexes in cities spawned factories, transport yards, rail loading stations, seaports, and staging areas for fabricated materials. As the American economy changed beginning in the 1960s and substantial components of manufacturing were lost to offshore competition or moved to more cost-efficient locations in other U.S. regions, many cities were left with the residue of empty industrial facilities.

As the American economy has evolved to include new functions, those activities require modern facilities suitable to new tasks. Manufacturing facilities in cities such as Pittsburgh and Youngstown, Ohio, for instance, have been torn down to make way for other uses. In other cases, they have been adapted for more modern uses. An obsolete General Motors factory in the San Fernando Valley section of Los Angeles is now "the Plant," a major retail center using some of the old structures. Areas of Los Angeles that once were traditional manufacturing districts have been transformed into modern logistical and distribution facilities to support the transporting of goods from the massive ports of Los Angeles and Long Beach to the interior of the nation. Adapted industrial facilities as well as newly developed facilities supported by computerized logistics technologies constitute a string of packaging sites along the Alameda Corridor, which expedites rail and truck transport from the ports.

Important components of manufacturing still exist in cities in the form of small shops and fabrication facilities called tier-two and tier-three suppliers to larger firms. Many of those suppliers have long histories in urban neighborhoods and have been nimble enough to adapt to new economic opportunities. Boston created an explicit economic development strategy, termed "the Back Streets Strategy," to support small manufacturers and supplier firms.

Several facets of the new economy also create the need for specialized industrial space. Entire sections of San Jose, California, are dedicated to the unique requirements of software development firms, technology research, and life sciences companies. Specialized industrial facilities may require ultra-clean rooms, specialized electronic support systems, and sophisticated data communication facilities. These constitute the new wave of industrial facilities that are required in the nation's urban areas as the new economy continues to evolve.

As international shipping and trade activity boosts demand for warehouse facilities at metropolitan seaports and airports, opportunities for investment in industrial space will increase. The field of logistics is changing rapidly. For example, technology is being applied to inventory management and to delivery logistics, putting a competitive premium on the speed of handling deliveries and therefore a premium on locations within population centers. In the near future, drones might regularly deliver goods to consumers. Also, because more cargo is moving by rail, new distribution facilities for large industrial complexes must be built along rail lines.

Another example emerges from the planned widening of the Panama Canal, which will allow larger ships to sail from Asia through the canal to the U.S. East Coast. Ports such as those at Norfolk, Virginia, and Savannah, Georgia, are deepening their docking points, with the result that greater volumes of cargo will be distributed from the East Coast. Patterns of transport will be altered and appropriate facilities must be built.

Recent investments at the ports in Los Angeles/Long Beach, San Francisco, and Seattle in the West; New York/New Jersey and Miami in the East; and Houston on the Gulf Coast are generating the need for a range of investments in logistical technologies.

Massive opportunities exist to invest in urban distribution facilities that incorporate the most advanced technologies in computerized logistics systems. For example, Amazon.com's evolving consumer information systems—which the company claims will allow it to anticipate customers' needs and start shipping items before they are purchased—will require specialized warehouses to stock goods next to cargo

HOTEL CALIFORNIA

During the early 1990s, the old financial and retail district of downtown Los Angeles was used as a movie set—for films about urban dystopia. A pastiche of abandoned buildings, some literally collapsing, provided the backdrop for denizens of skid row going about the dismal business of daily survival. An office construction boom during the 1980s in the skyscraper district adjacent to the old downtown had left office rents at historic lows, and it appeared the downtown was headed for even further decline.

Then came the Staples Center. The sports and entertainment arena was the subject of heated political debate over the investment of public funding. The project opened in 1999 adjacent to the Los Angeles Convention Center and was an immediate success in drawing the public back into downtown L.A. In the mid-2000s, it was joined by the development of L.A. Live, a 27-acre, $2.5 billion entertainment complex with movie theaters, restaurants, clubs, and a 54-story hotel/condominium complex featuring the JW Marriott and Ritz-Carlton brands. In 2012, ground was broken on two new hotels—a 23-story building containing a 174-room Courtyard by Marriott and a 218-room Residence by Marriott Inn—completing the full spectrum of Marriott brands at one site.

The JW Marriott and Ritz-Carlton hotel and condominium complex next to the Staples Center puts residents and visitors within walking distance of entertainment, restaurants, and sporting events.
PRAYITNO

airports. Specialized buildings for technology research and development and for life sciences laboratories also offer attractive urban industrial real estate options.

Hotels and Hospitality

Since their earliest formation in human history, cities have been gathering places for people to interact as traders, religious pilgrims, or simply visitors. Cities of all sizes continue to serve as assembly places for human interaction. A major dimension of real estate in cities includes hospitality facilities. Some cities, such as Orlando and San Diego, have worked hard to create tourist attractions that make them desirable as family destinations; others, like Salt Lake City and Minneapolis, have specialized roles as religious centers; and still others are entertainment capitals, such as Nashville, Los Angeles, and New Orleans. Sports events draw people from across states and regions, and cities have carefully expanded the role of sports. One city that has done this is Indianapolis, not only attracting professional sports teams but also serving as a headquarters for amateur sports.

The resulting real estate investments include the most luxurious of five-star hotels for upscale visitors and for business executives on expense accounts. Conference hotels represent a major segment of the hospitality industry in many cities, including facilities built on the grounds of convention complexes, as at McCormick Place in Chicago, and for business conferences adjacent to hub airports, such as at Dallas/Fort Worth International Airport. Business-center hotels focus on the support systems that traveling business people require, including extensive internet and teleconferencing equipment, specialized conference rooms, video equipment for presentations, and transportation support to and from flights.

Another type of urban hotel is that which is targeted to family travel, particularly adjacent to amusement parks and other tourist attractions. Cities have developed amusement facilities to expand their tourist appeal and have encouraged family hospitality facilities to support them. Examples include Anaheim and Disneyland, San Diego and SeaWorld, Orlando and Walt Disney World, and New Orleans and the year-round range of attractions there. Other urban hospitality facilities include less expensive suites properties and extended-stay hotels and motels.

Orlando and Disney World warrant further discussion, for they demonstrate how tourism can catalyze urban growth. The Walt Disney Company bought 27,000 acres of undeveloped swampland outside Orlando in 1965 and created Walt Disney World on that land. Despite efforts to prevent development in the areas surrounding the park—through the Reedy Creek Improvement District (Disney World's own private government with taxation, regulation, and development powers)—Disney World precipitated a wave of speculation and development in the Orlando metropolitan region that has yet to subside. Disney World itself has expanded, with other theme parks and studios as well as resort hotels and a shopping district. Today, Disney World attracts about 55 million visitors every year, which is more than any other U.S. city.

The hotel sector is a promising urban category as business trade and tourist travel continuously increase in the nation's metropolitan areas. To be competitive, hotel property owners and managers are applying new technologies to increase guest appeal and convenience. Some hotels offer iPads in order to provide newspapers and room-service menus digitally. Apps that enable guests to compare prices and reserve rooms are also important.

The critical hospitality property indicators have pointed in positive directions since the depths of the economic downturn. Occupancy levels, room rates, and revenues are positioned solidly for the next several years in major markets such as New York, San Francisco, and Los Angeles. In the fourth quarter of 2013, the New York market had more than 27,000 hotel rooms under construction—a volume equivalent to 25 percent of the city's total current supply of hotel rooms. Though luxury properties face the challenge of supporting continuous investment to maintain their status and extended-stay facilities seem to be oversupplied, good investment opportunities present themselves in business-center hotels in metropolitan areas where the new economy is surging. Furthermore, an undersupply exists in many cities because little new product has been added in recent years.[26] Specialized urban destination markets with business conferencing or family vacation reputations, such as San Antonio, Orlando, Dallas, and Chicago, can expect strong hotel prospects. Hotel performance correlates strongly with GDP growth, so the trajectory of the national economy toward metropolitan centers is significant for hospitality sector investments.

Urban Infrastructure

The emerging investment field of providing capital for infrastructure involves monetizing streams of revenue for toll roads, bridges, tunnels, airports, communication systems, electrical distribution and the "smart" grid, water and wastewater treatment, and renewable energy. These infrastructure needs are growing rapidly in scale and importance to the country. Cities will be the focal points of massive infrastructure expansions and modernization. For example,

FROM STUDENT PAPER TO FORTUNE 500

When Fred Smith wrote a student paper about the prospects for automating the package delivery business in the 1960s, Memphis, Tennessee, was known mostly for cotton, the blues, the nation's first supermarket (Piggly Wiggly), and, of course, Elvis Presley. Now it is also known for FedEx, the company Smith founded in 1971 in Little Rock, Arkansas, as Federal Express, so named because it was loosely modeled on the geographic logistical model pioneered by the Federal Reserve System, before moving it to Memphis in 1973.

FedEx is now the city's largest employer. Its "superhub" sorting and handling facilities occupy 15 million square feet on 862 acres at the Memphis International Airport, which—with FedEx's 196 aircraft gates—is the largest cargo air terminal in the world. The hub handles 2.2 million packages per day, or 160,000 packages and 265,000 documents per hour. These packages are moved on 42 miles of conveyor belts before being sent to one of the company's regional hubs, located in Indianapolis; Newark, New Jersey; Oakland, California; Fort Worth, Texas; Anchorage, Alaska; Miami; Toronto; Paris; Cologne, Germany; and Guangzhou, China.

Headquartered in Memphis, Tennessee, FedEx uses a regional logistical model similar to that used by the U.S. Federal Reserve to send millions of packages around the world each day.
FREDERIC LEGRAND-COMEO/SHUTTERSTOCK.COM

Mayor Rahm Emanuel worked to create the Chicago Infrastructure Trust to retrofit the city's aging buildings, bridges, and roads and to expand broadband access. Transportation infrastructure, including subways, bridges, and roads, is aging rapidly across the country and will cost cities more money in the long run if it is not upgraded soon.[27]

Though a modest first step, the Chicago Infrastructure Trust is trying to address a major truth: the United States is a metropolitan nation and needs smart urban infrastructure to sustain its competitiveness on a global scale. Global competitiveness in an increasingly interwoven economy requires infrastructure that will foster the accelerated growth of new-economy firms. That means broadening the definition of infrastructure beyond traditional categories to include modernized logistics systems and the infrastructure of information, such as data centers and media networks that instantaneously connect the productive capacities of society and which mobilize intellectual and physical inputs to the economy. At a microlevel, fiber-optic networks are making it possible to convert old manufacturing buildings into "maker spaces" such as in San Leandro, California, where multiple small firms collaborate to move through the phases from incubation to production by harnessing instantaneous communications.[28] Table 2 outlines the types of urban infrastructure facilities needed to support the nation's economy.

Technology will play a significant role in the development of more modernized infrastructure by introducing new levels of interactivity, price-driven choices, and efficiency. The nation's infrastructure model will not be based simply on building more of the same facilities or adding more volume, capacity, or size. Rather, it will focus on creating improved technology systems that introduce concepts of speed, responsiveness, and information-based decision making, leading to enhanced productivity. For example, technology applied to the installation of smart electrical grids transforms the relationship between electrical power generators/distributors and consumers into a process of feedback, decision making, and choices. Technology applied to the logistical chain expedites the movement of cargo from seaports via rail and air systems to consumers. Infrastructure built to these levels of sophistication will enable cities to support the nation's economic competitiveness.

A quote from the Urban Land Institute's *Infrastructure 2010* report underscores the significance of the sector: "The stakes are considerable. America's future prosperity, world economic standing, and ability to accommodate 100

TABLE 2: TYPES OF URBAN INFRASTRUCTURE

Transportation	Communication	Energy and utilities	Social infrastructure
Toll roads	Telephone systems	Energy generation	Universities
Bridges	Cell towers	Energy transmission	Schools
Tunnels	Cable networks	Renewable energy	Hospitals and health care facilities
Parking garages	Wi-fi	Natural gas pipeline and storage	Stadiums
Airports	Satellite	Gas storage and distribution	Convention facilities
Rail systems	Television	Local utilities	Student housing
Seaports	Radio	Water supply	Military housing
Transport		Wastewater treatment	Government-sponsored housing
Distribution centers			Corrections facilities
Urban mass transit			

VIA VERDE

Via Verde, a mixed-income residential development, is a key component of New York City's efforts to revitalize the south Bronx. The project features innovative, high-quality, sustainable design, and affordable rental and ownership housing for people in a range of income levels, combined with health-focused amenities.

Located on a remediated brownfield, Via Verde is a model for affordable, green, and healthy urban living. The project includes 222 mixed-income residential units, 7,500 square feet of retail and community space, and 40,000 square feet of green roofs and other open space for residents. The primary goal of the $98.8 million project was to provide a mix of rental and homeownership opportunities for people in a range of income levels to create a truly mixed-income community. A second goal was to address the community's health issues—particularly the rising levels of childhood asthma and obesity—

caused, in part, by the lack of opportunities for exercise and healthy eating.

A series of green roofs serves as the organizing architectural element and gives a unique identity to the development. The building steps up from three-story townhouses at the south end of the site to a 20-story tower at the north. South-facing solar panels generate power to light all common areas. The facade has prefabricated aluminum, cement, and wood panels, plus large windows, sunshades, and courtyard-facing balconies. Via Verde offers a healthier lifestyle to an urban neighborhood, with a rooftop vegetable garden, space for outdoor activity, and an indoor fitness facility. A Montefiore Medical Center wellness facility and a pharmacy occupy ground-floor space.

The name Via Verde means "green way" in Spanish and refers to the green rooftops connected by stairways that wind upward from the ground-level courtyard.

Via Verde was instrumental in reviving the south Bronx neighborhood of New York City.
JONATHAN ROSE COMPANIES

million more people by 2050 directly depend on bolstering its primary economic gateway cities and metropolitan regions, which produce 90 percent of the nation's GDP. The challenge necessitates integrating housing, transportation, water, and energy with land use in a comprehensive way. Delay promises only the prospect of steadily ebbing vitality as the world order now begins to pass America by as countries in the European Union and Asia, in particular China, continue to implement policies to integrate railroad transit, airport, and seaport networks to serve major economic hubs using 21st-century technologies and systems."[29]

Substantial opportunities exist in public/private infrastructure investing, which is at the

earliest stages of development in the United States. Investors in Australia and Europe have demonstrated that combining public and private resources can produce major infrastructure improvements and generate strong long-term, inflation-hedged returns.

Urban Multifamily Rental

The urban multifamily sector covers a wide range of apartment configurations. It includes small, individually owned structures, such as duplexes and fourplexes, as well as larger garden apartments and high-rise buildings in larger cities. The multifamily sector is classified according to the quality of buildings, rental price points, and vintage. Class A is the highest category of apartment communities; Class B is a lesser-quality category; and Class C often includes governmentally subsidized rentals.

In the largest and most robust real estate markets, rental housing is the residence of choice for young professionals. Many rental units exist in high rises in cities such as New York, Boston, San Francisco, and Chicago. They make dense concentrations of populations possible and generate support for urban amenities such as neighborhood restaurants and shops of all kinds.

In cities where high-rise residential buildings are not the norm, however, garden apartments are the primary choice for renters. They typically are two- or three-story structures with exterior entrances and ground-level parking adjacent to the units or podium parking underneath the living units. Such apartment complexes frequently offer amenities such as swimming pools, exercise rooms, barbecue patios, and community rooms.

A major challenge in the rental sector is affordability. In most metropolitan areas, a family earning the minimum wage cannot afford the fair market rent on a two-bedroom apartment, according to the Low Income Housing Coalition. The influx of tech companies into the San Francisco Bay area, for example, has caused the housing market to become more competitive and rents to surge, driving middle- and working-class families out of the city. A pressing need exists for more affordable supply, for local policies to produce affordable units, and for national policies that strike a balance between support for homeownership and for rental units.

In most cities, affordable rental housing does not take the form of high-rise buildings. A notable exception is New York City, where high-rise structures for working families have been the norm for many years. Another exception is public housing, although recent design innovations under the HOPE VI program have put an emphasis on smaller-scale, less dense developments. In

many cities, assisted housing for seniors is also in high rises. In the evolving urban future, the principal way to develop units within affordable ranges in many cities will be to opt for greater density in various configurations.

In many urban areas, a significant source of multifamily rentals is federally subsidized housing programs. One such program is public housing, a source of thousands of units of affordable rentals in most metropolitan areas. Public housing is managed by local public housing authorities, and typically about half of the units managed by the authorities are publicly owned units in developments and the other half are privately owned apartments rented through portable Section 8 vouchers. Many of the most deteriorated units in projects have been dramatically renovated in recent years through HOPE VI (now continuing under the more comprehensive Choice Neighborhoods program). The focus has been on creating lower-density projects while achieving a degree of income integration by including market-rate rental units in the mix of housing and by attracting private investment.

Section 8 is a program that depends on the participation of private apartment owners. It provides a subsidy to property owners who provide rental units to eligible tenants. The Section 8 program may take the form of subsidies assigned to each individual tenant or can be provided for new construction directly to the developer as project-based Section 8.

One of the nation's most successful programs for generating affordable rentals is the Low Income Housing Tax Credit Program. It provides a subsidy through tax credits apportioned to state housing finance agencies. The competition among developers at the local level to be assigned tax credits has resulted in high-quality projects, creative designs, and well-managed rental facilities for low-income families, disabled persons, and seniors. The federal government also supports a range of specialized programs for seniors, principally under its 202

Program, which have resulted in thousands of high-quality apartments for older Americans.

The strongest real estate investment sector in today's urban economy is multifamily rental. When surveyed, a strong majority of investors say their preferred real estate sector is apartments.[30] This dominance is in large measure because of tremendous pent-up demand fueled by household growth, including young professionals who have been living with their parents and are steadily moving to live independently as the job market improves. The nation's growing immigrant population is largely made up of apartment dwellers. And as the nation's homeownership rate drops from 69 percent to stabilize at a projected 65 percent, every one-point drop in the homeownership rate represents about 1.1 million people who need to be housed and whose likeliest residential recourse is apartments. Creative approaches will be needed to build rental units for aging Americans who want to live independently, for university students in urban areas, and for the families of military personnel.

Two-thirds of the new households formed over the next decade will be renters, which translates into 6 million new renter households. With insufficient supply having been built during the Great Recession, the result is a mismatch between supply and demand that will last for a number of years because of lag times in the building process. Apartment absorption will be at high levels for several years. The result will be favorable investment opportunities in the retrofitting of existing units as well as in the development of new supply. Caution must be exercised, however, to avoid overbuilding or overpricing as massive amounts of capital are deployed to the dynamic rental sector. The operative conditions for apartments to continue their strength as a sector in the years ahead include favorable cap rates, attractive apartment unit prices, and improved occupancy in metropolitan markets across the nation.

CHAPTER 3

Categorizing Cities by Real Estate Potential

Dallas is ranked sixth in the 2014 Regions to Watch Index. Its economic and demographic measures suggest a strong economic future for the city.
THOMAS MCCONNELL

As important as evaluations of property types are to real estate decisions, so too are assessments of the strengths of metropolitan areas—that is, the cities and regions in which the investments and building will occur. A metropolitan area's overall economic vitality bears heavily on the prospects for success of individual projects, and it also influences the attitudes of debt and equity sources. The general strength of the metropolitan economy

by the Urban Land Institute and PwC published in *Emerging Trends in Real Estate® 2014*. It ranks 51 metropolitan areas by the assessments of investors, developers, and builders concerning the 2014 prospects for those markets.

These two charts show that while the quantitative measures and expert opinions generally coalesce into the similar groupings of cities, divergences exist. For example, San Francisco scores 21st in the quantitative rankings but is ranked first in the survey; and New York City, which scores only 34th in the quantitative measures, ranks fourth in the survey. On the other hand, Oklahoma City, which scores eighth in the quantitative rankings, is assessed at 43rd by the survey respondents.

Several factors may explain these discrepancies. One is that the investors may be focusing on specific opportunities, such as certain submarkets or even individual projects within their areas of specialization. Such opportunities might well be seen as attractive investments, even with mixed quantitative measures for a region as a whole. That could certainly be true in markets as large and diverse as San Francisco and New York. Another explanation may be that expert opinions are formed from high-profile past successes in such markets and not based on regional measures. And finally, experts from the most prominent real estate groups may simply be more familiar with and more confident about the large, well-established metro areas and the larger number of opportunities they present and tend to discount the lesser scale of projects and the narrower range of options in robust smaller markets such as Oklahoma City.

Merged Groupings of Metro Areas

By merging the two rankings—one a quantitative listing and the other an opinion survey—it is possible to find a degree of consensus about workable groupings of the 45 metropolitan areas that appear in both rankings. For real

U.S. MARKETS TO WATCH: OVERALL REAL ESTATE PROSPECTS

1 San Francisco (2/1/1)	6.98	6.88	7.74
2 Houston (1/3/2)	7.00	6.64	7.48
3 San Jose (5/2/3)	6.78	6.75	7.40
4 New York City (3/4/6)	6.84	6.58	7.19
5 Dallas/Fort Worth (6/6/4)	6.76	6.37	7.36
6 Seattle (4/7/7)	6.83	6.36	7.19
7 Austin (7/10/5)	6.69	6.25	7.34
8 Miami (10/5/8)	6.57	6.38	7.06
9 Boston (8/8/9)	6.64	6.35	6.87
10 Orange County, CA (9/12/10)	6.60	6.17	6.85
11 Denver (13/14/11)	6.46	6.15	6.84
12 Nashville (14/11/15)	6.46	6.18	6.75
13 Los Angeles (15/13/17)	6.45	6.15	6.70
14 San Antonio (19/16/12)	6.28	6.10	6.79
15 San Diego (12/19/16)	6.47	5.91	6.71
16 Charlotte (17/18/13)	6.37	5.92	6.79
17 Raleigh/Durham (18/20/14)	6.31	5.90	6.79
18 Salt Lake City (16/17/19)	6.42	6.03	6.54
19 Portland, OR (11/21/25)	6.53	5.88	6.28
20 Minneapolis/St. Paul (20/9/26)	6.27	6.27	5.91
21 Chicago (22/15/27)	6.11	6.11	5.89
22 Washington, D.C. (26/26/18)	5.88	5.46	6.54
23 Tampa/St. Petersburg (24/22/23)	5.97	5.59	6.30
24 Orlando (25/23/21)	5.89	5.56	6.40
25 Phoenix (21/28/24)	6.14	5.41	6.29
26 Atlanta (23/27/22)	6.05	5.43	6.33
27 Northern New Jersey (28/31/20)	5.85	5.25	6.40
28 Inland Empire (27/24/28)	5.87	5.53	5.73
29 Honolulu/Hawaii (29/25/30)	5.68	5.46	5.56
30 Philadelphia (30/33/31)	5.56	5.04	5.56
31 Indianapolis (34/29/35)	5.33	5.33	5.40
32 Pittsburgh (31/37/37)	5.55	4.90	5.29
33 Westchester/Fairfield (33/39/33)	5.48	4.82	5.43
34 Virginia Beach/Norfolk (36/36/29)	5.21	4.91	5.58
35 Kansas City (35/30/43)	5.28	5.28	5.11
36 St. Louis (37/32/42)	5.18	5.18	5.13
37 Baltimore (38/40/36)	5.15	4.74	5.31
38 Las Vegas (32/43/41)	5.49	4.44	5.15
39 Jacksonville (42/42/34)	4.96	4.64	5.42
40 Sacramento (40/44/32)	5.05	4.43	5.53
41 Cincinnati (41/34/44)	4.98	4.98	4.92
42 Columbus (43/35/46)	4.94	4.94	4.81
43 Oklahoma City (45/41/39)	4.82	4.67	5.18
44 Tucson (39/47/38)	5.14	4.28	5.19
45 Milwaukee (44/38/47)	4.83	4.83	4.70
46 Albuquerque (46/45/40)	4.65	4.33	5.18
47 New Orleans (48/46/45)	4.49	4.30	4.83
48 Memphis (47/49/48)	4.52	4.07	4.49
49 Cleveland (50/48/50)	4.20	4.20	4.00
50 Providence, RI (49/50/49)	4.30	3.66	4.30
51 Detroit (51/51/51)	3.12	3.12	2.96

Source: *Emerging Trends in Real Estate®* 2014 survey.
Note: Numbers in parentheses are rankings for, in order, investment, development, and homebuilding.

estate decision-making purposes, and because the creation of numerical rankings is more art than science, the precise numerical ranking of a city may not be as useful as the general grouping within which a metropolitan area can be assessed as a starting point for further analyses. That general sense enables the start of the much more detailed study, which is required to make important investment decisions. Table 5 presents those metro areas that appear in both analyses in four categories based on their combined scores. The metropolitan areas are listed alphabetically within each category.

Cities are organized into four categories: 1) consensus strongest, 2) mixed rankings with strong measures, 3) mixed rankings with weak measures, and 4) consensus weakest. A closer look at the trajectories of the metropolitan areas in each of the four groupings reveals common themes that can help explain their relative forward momentum or their lagging conditions. For example, the 12 cities in the consensus strongest grouping each have broad-based economies with strengths in the fastest growth sectors of the national economy. Eleven of the 12 have demonstrated significant job growth in advanced industries, which are characterized by high research and development spending and by high proportions of employees in the science, technology, engineering, and mathematics (STEM) fields. Advanced industries include manufacturing—such as computer equipment, industrial machinery, and pharmaceuticals—as well as service sectors, such as software and computer systems. These industries generate well-paying jobs in strong supply chains and stimulate local economies. They also apply technology and innovation to traditional industries, such as the telecommunications sector in Dallas, the energy sector in Houston, and health care in Nashville, where accelerating employment expansions are fueled by advanced industries, such as energy, technology, and automotive.

Consensus Strongest

▶ Austin: Advanced industries, state capital, Texas Triangle
▶ Dallas/Fort Worth: Advanced industries, Texas Triangle
▶ Denver: Advanced industries, state capital
▶ Houston: Advanced industries, Texas Triangle
▶ Nashville: State capital

TABLE 5: MERGING OF DEMOGRAPHIC/ECONOMIC INDICATORS AND SURVEY ASSESSMENTS FOR 45 METROPOLITAN AREAS

Consensus strongest	Mixed rankings with strong measures	Mixed rankings with weak measures	Consensus weakest
Austin	Baltimore	Atlanta	Cincinnati
Dallas/Fort Worth	Boston	Chicago	Cleveland
Denver	Charlotte	Columbus	Detroit
Houston	Indianapolis	Kansas City	Jacksonville
Nashville	Minneapolis/St. Paul	Los Angeles	Las Vegas
Portland	Miami	New Orleans	Memphis
Raleigh	New York	Orlando	Milwaukee
Salt Lake City	Oklahoma City	Philadelphia	Providence
San Antonio	Phoenix	Tampa/St. Petersburg	Sacramento
San Francisco	Pittsburgh	Virginia Beach/Norfolk	St. Louis
San Jose	San Diego		
Seattle	Washington, D.C.		

CONSENSUS STRONGEST

- ▶ Portland: Advanced industries
- ▶ Raleigh: Advanced industries, state capital
- ▶ Salt Lake City: Advanced industries, state capital
- ▶ San Antonio: Advanced industries, Texas Triangle
- ▶ San Francisco: Advanced industries
- ▶ San Jose: Advanced industries
- ▶ Seattle: Advanced industries

Five of the 12 cities in the consensus strongest category are state capitals, where government jobs create bases of employment and salary stability. Four of the 12 are in the economically robust Texas Triangle—Houston, Dallas, Austin, and San Antonio—where state policies support globally competitive economic development. Eight of the 12 metropolitan areas are in the "sun and sand" states, which continue to attract in-migration above the national average.

AUSTIN

An exemplar of the consensus strongest group, Austin has been listed among the nation's met-ropolitan growth leaders for decades. Now, it is generally accepted as the undisputed pacesetter among those cities that balance impressive technology-driven economic development with stimulating urban environments. A metropolitan area long ambiguous in its support for urban growth is now leading the nation in many key measures of economic expansion. In 2007–2012 Austin's regional GDP increased by 31.7 percent, and in 2007–2013 its job growth increased by 11.8 percent—both the highest measures among metropolitan areas in the nation.

Over the last several decades, Austin has built upon its early technology assets, such as a 1960s-vintage IBM presence (still one of the city's largest employers), and steadily built a broad platform of globally significant technology research, development, and production companies. Harnessing the momentum of local startups that have grown to worldwide stature—such as Dell—and globally established companies that want to be near Austin's complex of technology assets—such as Google—Austin has built a dynamic sector of advanced industries to complement its traditional economic engines of state government, higher education, and tourism. Austin's critical mass of assets revolves around the world-class University of Texas at Austin and the amenities and activities that help retain high-performing students after their university years and which attract creative, lifestyle-oriented young professionals from around the world.

Austin may well be at an inflection point where its well-established technology reputation is being applied to step up to even higher-level opportunities. For example, the commitment of the University of Texas to establish a new health sciences center in Austin is intended to foster entrepreneurial combinations that can accelerate the growth of biotechnology companies. And underscoring the city's attractiveness to technology executives from around the world is the decision of Virgin Airlines to begin nonstop flights from Austin to London.

Tempering this rising economic trajectory is the fact that the steady growth of recent decades presents serious infrastructure challenges for the Austin region. Highway congestion is severe after years of inaction concerning needed arterials and freeways. Austin's leaders must ensure available reserves of competitively priced electrical power for energy-intensive data centers and ample long-term water supplies in a water-scarce state. Private investment opportunities present themselves in

Real estate development in Austin, Texas, continues to be strong despite the downturn during the Great Recession. Austin leads the nation in GDP and job growth largely due to the continuing success of its tech industry.
DELL INC./WIKIMEDIA COMMONS

alternative-energy projects, water transactions, creative transportation strategies, and in solutions to other infrastructure concerns.

Real Estate Investment Potential. The investment outlook is positive for forward-looking forms of real estate investment. The accelerating growth of startup companies and the demand for business and professional services to support them will drive a continuing market for downtown office space, office parks, and research campuses. Business travel, as well as Austin's role as a music and entertainment center, will sustain lifestyle hospitality projects. Industrial space with modern logistical technology is needed along Interstate 35—the North American Free Trade Agreement (NAFTA) corridor—in the region from San Marcos south of Austin to beyond Round Rock in the north. The continuing attraction of young professionals who are characterized by career mobility and preferences for stimulating and walkable living environments means that there will be continuing demand for apartments and other urban housing types, with creative designs and amenity packages near technology employers and adjacent to entertainment nodes. And the demographic patterns of growing populations of minority residents (particularly American Latino households), of immigrants, and of relocating U.S. residents will sustain the for-sale home market among the strongest in the nation.

Austin's population increase of 6.3 percent from 2007 to 2012 was the fastest in the nation, and the domestic migration rate of 17 percent was also the highest. New residential investment opportunities are presented by Austin's burgeoning central business district, including major high-rise condo buildings that together contribute both to population density in the downtown and to a striking city skyline.

Each one of these forms of real estate investment will require investors to be attentive to design and sustainability considerations that respect the sensitive character of the Hill Country's physical environment as well as take into account the local government's stringent attention to environmental concerns.

Mixed Rankings with Strong Measures

▶ Baltimore: Legacy industries
▶ Boston: Legacy industries, state capital
▶ Charlotte: Affected industries
▶ Indianapolis: Legacy industries, state capital
▶ Minneapolis/St. Paul: Legacy industries, state capital
▶ Miami: Housing recession overhang
▶ New York City: Affected industries
▶ Oklahoma City: Housing recession overhang, state capital
▶ Phoenix: Housing recession overhang, state capital
▶ Pittsburgh: Legacy industries
▶ San Diego: Housing recession overhang
▶ Washington, D.C.: Affected industries, national capital

The metro areas in the second grouping—i.e., those with mixed rankings but with many strong measures—tend to have urban economies historically concentrated in slower-growing industries. While legacy industries—steel mills and similar manufacturing industries—have by and large vanished from the industrial Midwest, turning the region into the Rust Belt, the vestiges of those industries still hang over cities like Pittsburgh and Indianapolis.

Despite having economies transitioning to include significant shares of growth industries, four of the 12 metro areas in this category are challenged by historic concentrations of older industries in decline. Thus, Baltimore, Boston, Indianapolis, and Pittsburgh must continue the transformations of their employment bases.

Other metro areas in this group have large shares of important national sectors, but sectors that were battered by the recession. For example, Charlotte's national banking centers and New York's financial institutions retrenched significantly during the recession and have not

returned to previous levels of employment. Cities such as Miami and Phoenix were at the epicenter of the housing downturn, in states that were among the hardest hit—Florida and Arizona, respectively—and have taken several years to recover.

Five of the metro areas in this category have strong economic foundations associated with their roles as state capitals and, in the case of the Washington, D.C., region, as the nation's capital. Most of the metro areas in this category are also using foresighted strategies of engaging first-class institutions of higher education to accelerate their economic transformations.

BALTIMORE

Baltimore is a city steeped in some of the most revered episodes of American history. It is Fort McHenry in Baltimore Harbor where, in the words of the U.S. national anthem, "that star-spangled banner yet wave." The city has also played a key role in the nation's economic history, with its contributions to Atlantic shipping, its steel mills, its breweries, and the tool factories that helped define the industrial era.

In a cruel twist of economic history, Baltimore's neighborhoods and inner suburbs are also emblematic of the deindustrialization that battered America's urban economies beginning in the 1960s. In Baltimore, as in other cities across the country, factories closed, plants moved offshore, manufacturing moved to the outer suburbs, jobs were lost, neighborhoods declined in population, and the nation labeled these outcomes an "urban crisis." In fact, it was a transition far more extensive than just an urban transition. The nation's industrial composition had shifted; and while the financial capital, the personnel positions, and the manufacturing equipment could be moved, the vacant real estate and the deteriorated buildings in cities like Baltimore were the residue that could not be shipped away.

As the employment base eroded, the social costs accumulated. Large numbers of Baltimore's residents followed the jobs, leaving behind neighborhoods of concentrated poverty. The result was a cycle of unemployment, crime, and poorly performing schools. In Baltimore, heroic efforts by municipal leaders and civic organizations helped the city cope. Developer James Rouse converted the Inner Harbor into a nationally noted "people place," even as his nonprofit creation, the Enterprise Foundation, uplifted core neighborhoods such as Sandtown-Winchester. Several mayoral administrations managed the replacement of all of Baltimore's high-rise public housing developments with less dense, attractive new urbanist communities decentralized across the city. Prodigious civic efforts focused on public school performance, youth employment, crime reduction, housing preservation, financial counseling, and economic development.

Baltimore's economy and physical landscape are being recycled, but it has required a long and wrenching transition to a new economy to finance the conversion of obsolete manufacturing floor space to new business incubators and to engineer the adaptation of vacant factories into sunlit lofts for the creative class. Impressive gains are reflected in Baltimore's educational attainment improvement from 2007 to 2012, which was third among all metro areas in the United States. Baltimore's transition has been 40 years in the making, and even now it is uneven. But more than many other American cities that are going through similar transformations, Baltimore has assets to build upon.

Baltimore is blessed in that it sits at one end of a corridor—the Baltimore–Washington Corridor—that is home to federal governmental institutions that invest in some of the most promising advanced industries of the new economy. For example, communications and technology firms are drawn to the massive federal cybersecurity campuses along I-95 in Maryland. The

multiple national health institutes in the region combine their world-class research capabilities with those of the Johns Hopkins Medical Center and the University of Maryland Medical School in Baltimore's core city to create one of the nation's premier life sciences complexes. Civic drivers such as the Annie E. Casey Foundation are designing plans for small-business incubators to harness the potential of the region's biomedical assets in Baltimore's neighborhoods. The Baltimore region's GDP grew by 8.2 percent from 2007 to 2012 and its job growth increased by 1.9 percent from 2007 to 2013—both measures in the top third of all U.S. metro areas. Both within the core city and in the region, opportu-

The mixed-use design of the University of Maryland BioPark will connect the facility to Baltimore's famed Inner Harbor and will complement the walkable nature of development around the harbor.
UNIVERSITY OF MARYLAND AT BALTIMORE

nities exist for real estate investors to build upon the new economic growth and employment expansion.

Real Estate Investment Potential. Viewed through an investor's lens, Baltimore today is a textbook example of how America's urban landscape can be recycled as new economic functions evolve. Historic buildings can be adapted to new uses, obsolete structures can be demolished, land can be cleared for modern purposes, and state-of-the-art designs and engineering can produce new public facilities, residential developments, and commercial projects that are attractive, sustainable, and successful.

Particular attention has been paid to the city's west-side neighborhood, located next to the central business district. The Baltimore Development Corporation has helped build a partnership between the private sector, the University of Maryland, and the city of Baltimore to redevelop "the former retail district into a vibrant downtown neighborhood of office, educational, arts, health care, and residential uses."[31] The vision is to create an urban mixed-use neighborhood, composed of 100 square blocks that connect to the central downtown area, universities, historic residential neighborhoods, and the Inner Harbor. The 12-acre University of Maryland BioPark works toward those ends by uniting science companies and the university's various research centers and activities to spur innovation and economic development. Located on the west side of the University of Maryland campus, the BioPark will span 1.8 million square feet of space upon buildout.

Mixed Rankings with Weak Measures

▶ Atlanta: Housing recession overhang, advanced industries, state capital
▶ Chicago: Legacy industries
▶ Columbus: Legacy industries, state capital
▶ Kansas City: Legacy industries
▶ Los Angeles: Recession overhang, advanced industries
▶ New Orleans: Postdisaster effects
▶ Orlando: Housing recession overhang
▶ Philadelphia: Legacy industries
▶ Tampa/St. Petersburg: Housing recession overhang
▶ Virginia Beach/Norfolk: Affected industries

While the internal dynamics of the ten metro areas in the third category—those with mixed rankings but with higher shares of weak measures—are in many respects similar to those of the metro areas in the previous category, on close examination it is clear that they have more negative trends that push them into this grouping.

Metro areas in this category include those that are in regions that were hit very hard by the housing recession, such as Orlando and Tampa/St. Petersburg in Florida and Atlanta in Georgia. Four of the ten are challenged by large shares of legacy industries in the Rust Belt: Chicago, Columbus, Kansas City, and Philadelphia. Another—New Orleans—is in a region that suffered severe blows from Hurricane Katrina and the BP oil spill in the Gulf of Mexico. Each of the ten cities in this grouping has clear strengths and has been a national urban leader in the past. As they reestablish stability after the setbacks of recent years and engage their unique strengths, any of these metro areas can reverse the trends that placed them in a category characterized by weak performance measures.

LOS ANGELES

Los Angeles is a study in contrasts. Viewed from one perspective, it is a Pacific Rim center of capital flows, a global hotbed of new media, and a shipping and packaging node for massive volumes of cargo entering the United States. These economic functions generate jobs, wealth, and real estate opportunities. But viewed from another vantage point, the city includes many square miles of poor neighborhoods where crime rates are high.

Without a doubt, Los Angeles is a global economic powerhouse. It is home to large shares of some of the most important and highest-growth sectors of the new American economy. The ports of Los Angeles/Long Beach as well as Los Angeles International Airport funnel high-value cargo to packaging and distribution points via the Alameda Corridor. The region is home

MIXED RANKINGS WITH WEAK MEASURES

to highly ranked large research universities, including University of California, Los Angeles; the University of Southern California; and Cal Tech. Its medical centers are regarded as among the best in the world in virtually every specialty. Los Angeles is the unquestioned world capital of the traditional film and music industries, and those creative juggernauts have expanded to the new-media realms of electronic games, social networking, and media-related advanced industries. That creative complex, in turn, drives millions of visitors to theme parks, art districts, broadcast venues, and entertainment events of all types. Each of these economic activities creates demand for large-scale and continuous real estate investments.

In recent years, however, Los Angeles has suffered economic setbacks. Largely unnoticed amid the attention to its Hollywood image is the fact that for decades Los Angeles was a major manufacturing hub for industries as diverse as textiles, furniture, and computers. The region

had massive employment bases in the aerospace and defense product industries, which declined with the end of the Cold War and with more recent defense budget reductions. Thousands of well-paying jobs ended and enormous plants sat idle in wounded communities.

On the heels of those losses came the dot-com bust of 2000 and the housing-induced recession of 2007, during which real estate values in southern California dropped by 50 percent in some submarkets, among the most severe declines in the nation. From 2007 to 2013, the jobs base in Los Angeles declined by 4.6 percent, the ninth-poorest performance among the 52 metro areas measured in the Praxis Strategy Group study, while the region's unemployment rate of 8.9 percent in 2013 was the fifth highest among metro areas in the nation.

In 2013, the Los Angeles City Council established an independent commission—the Los Angeles 2020 Commission—to study the city's fiscal stability. The commission's *A Time for Truth*

The sprawling Los Angeles metropolitan area offers ample real estate investment opportunities throughout its many submarkets.

report found that Los Angeles has a jobs crisis and also struggles with persistent budget shortfalls, and that traffic dissuades employers from locating in the city. By 2014, the region's unemployment had fallen to 7.7 percent, ranking it sixth highest among large metro areas.[32]

Real Estate Investment Potential. The real estate investment climate in Los Angeles continues to be challenged by exorbitant prices for scarce developable land, by sprawling distances made more daunting by legendary traffic congestion, and by the low incomes of large segments of its immigrant communities. Yet the opportunities for strong returns from real estate investing are many. Foreign investors generate small businesses and create markets for offices, retail plazas, and residences. Local business startups in media, the biosciences, and profes-

sional services constitute new tenants for office and industrial parks. The region's year-round pleasant climate and its stimulating amenities draw in-migrants from across the nation and immigrants from around the world. That inflow of motivated, creative, and often financially capable populations translates into demand for apartments and homes at all price ranges.

It is important for real estate investors to note that the Los Angeles area is truly an aggregation of multiple submarkets, many of which approach populations of half a million. As a result, real estate investment opportunities vary with the economic life cycles and fortunes of subregions as diverse as San Pedro and the port areas, the west side, the beach communities, downtown Los Angeles (which has notably experienced a development boom in recent years), the South Bay, the San Fernando Valley, the Hollywood Hills, the San Gabriel Valley, and the Inland Empire. Significant cities such as Long Beach, Santa Monica, Glendale, Pasadena, Burbank, Beverly

Hills, and Ontario are interspersed across the Los Angeles Basin. And beyond Los Angeles, investment opportunities abound in adjacent Orange County and in San Diego County. Together with Los Angeles County, the three counties constitute a southern California complex that, if ranked among the economies of nations, would be the 15th-largest economy in the world.

Consensus Weakest

▶ Cincinnati: Legacy industries
▶ Cleveland: Legacy industries
▶ Detroit: Legacy industries
▶ Jacksonville: Housing recession overhang
▶ Las Vegas: Housing recession overhang
▶ Memphis: Legacy industries
▶ Milwaukee: Legacy industries
▶ Providence: Legacy industries, state capital
▶ Sacramento: Housing recession overhang, state capital
▶ St. Louis: Legacy industries

The ten metropolitan areas in the fourth category—the consensus weakest group—each have substantial challenges to overcome, yet still offer potential for creative investors.

Seven of the ten metro areas in this category have economies in which traditional industries have experienced decades of steep declines: Cincinnati, Cleveland, Detroit, Memphis, Milwaukee, Providence, and St. Louis. The American Assembly has labeled cities with these attributes as "legacy cities" because they struggle with older industrial bases, obsolete physical sites, and sunk legacy costs. Each of these metro areas lost jobs between 2007 and 2013—an average job loss of almost 5 percent—and each is striving to identify advanced industry growth sectors to replace declining industries. Cleveland, for example, has become a center of investment in medical device companies spawned by entrepreneurs who seek to tap the biosciences expertise at the Cleveland Clinic and Case Western

CONSENSUS WEAKEST

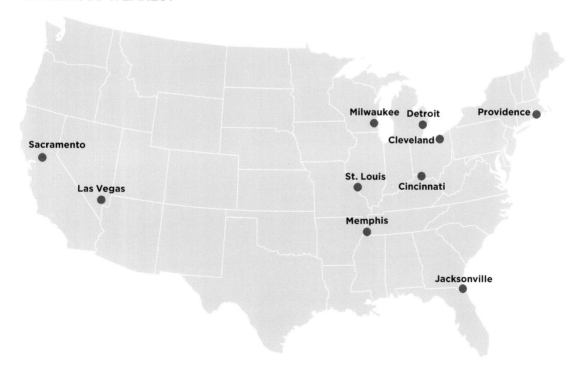

Reserve University. St. Louis also has biomedical assets, including the research capabilities within its large food product companies. In order to reverse the declines of recent decades, however, these seven metro areas must address histories of troubled school systems, the fiscal effects of long-term public sector revenue contractions, and slow or negative population growth.

Three of the metropolitan areas in this grouping—Las Vegas, Jacksonville, and Sacramento—are struggling to overcome the fact that the states and regions of which they are part were focal points of the housing crisis and the economic recession.

DETROIT

The Praxis Strategy Group report ranked 52 metropolitan areas based on eight economic and demographic measures. Detroit ranked among the lowest ten metro areas in seven of the eight statistical categories. Its metropolitan population loss from 2007 to 2012 was the most acute among all 52 metro areas, with the central city of Detroit continuing six decades of population decline from its population peak of 1.85 million in 1950 to approximately 700,000 today. The metro area's unemployment rate of 9.7 percent in 2013 was the second highest in the nation and its 6 percent decline in GDP from 2007 to 2012 was the fourth most precipitous of the 52. How did the acknowledged center of America's industrial capacity—once the richest city in the United States—decline so tragically?

During the 1940s, President Franklin Delano Roosevelt predicted that the United States would prevail in World War II because of its "arsenal of

The headquarters of Quicken Loans overlooks the redeveloped Campus Martius Park in the heart of downtown Detroit. Affordable land and strong anchor institutions create many investment opportunities in the Motor City.
NATHAN WEBER

democracy," thus describing the nation's prodigious capabilities to produce the tanks, aircraft, and ships needed to counter the Axis powers. Detroit's auto-making factories were converted to war purposes and rolled out hundreds of thousands of tanks and trucks and tens of thousands of aircraft.

At the end of the war, America stood as the industrial colossus of the world and Detroit made ready to produce the automobiles that would satiate the new-car appetites of America's expanding middle class. The car culture of the 1950s and 1960s drove demand for family station wagons, muscle cars, stretch luxury cars, and finned convertibles, and for creative designs for autos of unheard-of shapes and colors.

Metropolitan Detroit's massive concentration of employment and investment in automotive manufacturing, however, was precisely what made it vulnerable to the global economic forces and to the domestic social and political upheavals of the last four decades of the 20th century. The rise of competitor manufacturing nations and the failure of the car companies to adapt to consumer tastes and prices stunted the American automotive sector. Over the span of four decades, central Detroit went from being home to 15 auto factories to having only three. Its jobs base eroded, its neighborhoods deteriorated, its fiscal condition declined, and its race relations unraveled. The Detroit metropolitan area was on a sliding slope, and central city Detroit was in an even steeper spiral.

The Great Recession accelerated that downward spiral. General Motors declared bankruptcy, nascent plans for developments were terminated, foreclosures accumulated, a mayoral administration ended in prison sentences, and the city of Detroit was placed into state receivership. Detroit today is a city that houses less than 40 percent of the people that it did in 1950 on the same amount of land. The result is a panorama of abandoned houses, vacant lots, and shells of industrial buildings. A 2014 report by the Detroit Blight Removal Task Force documents more than 78,000 dilapidated or at-risk buildings—about 30 percent of the city's total—and 114,000 vacant lots.

Real Estate Investment Potential

From a real estate investment standpoint, the immense task of rebuilding Detroit seems insurmountable. Some urban experts caution against even attempting traditional approaches to revitalization and advise instead a radically different strategy. They argue for intentional downsizing, ceding vacant lots to adjacent owners and to community organizations and converting vast expanses of land into park space or even farmland. They suggest concentrating population in the more stable neighborhoods so that public safety and other basic municipal services can be provided efficiently in a smaller footprint.

Others argue that real estate market dynamics will recognize inexpensive, available land and low rents and attract entrepreneurs and investors. Evidence of investment opportunities exists in the accumulating wave of startup businesses, technology incubators, and creative studios acting upon the attraction of affordable spaces. In addition, major national investors, such as Dan Gilbert of Quicken Financial, are assembling major properties in downtown Detroit. They are banking on the resurgent potential of the central business district based on anchors such as the headquarters of a stabilized and profitable General Motors, public investment in major league sports facilities, and an expanding casino complex. The automotive complex is increasingly incorporating the technology innovations of advanced industries that draw upon the Detroit region's educational assets in engineering and other STEM fields.

Equally hope-inspiring is the coalescence of leadership institutions dedicated to bringing Detroit back from its low point. Federal assistance has been significant, the state of Michigan is shepherding the bankruptcy process, national corporations such as J.P. Morgan Chase are committing to the city's economic recovery, regional and national foundations such as the Kresge Foundation are focusing grants, and the nonprofit sector is mobilizing.

The challenges this coalition of leadership faces extend far beyond land use and real estate investment. They include sustaining essential public services, keeping schools open, improving workforce readiness, and stemming the population exodus. Detroit today is the place that will most dramatically test the question of whether a great American city will be allowed to slide into oblivion. The resources of the Detroit metropolitan region are still immense. Whether the leadership of the region can unify around effective strategies, create political will, and adhere to a consistent course over time will determine whether Detroit can become an example of survival and rebirth for other cities struggling with wrenching global change.

The four categories of cities developed from the merging of a quantitative assessment and an opinion survey help us understand cities in relationship to one another. Such a merging allows us to identify patterns across urban communities, across a variety of data points, and across studies with varying methodologies. Although this method is not an exact science, the development of broad categories in which to place major cities lays the foundation for the further analysis needed to make wise investment decisions and provides a critical snapshot of the economic vitality of America's key cities.

CHAPTER 4

Investment Strategies and Capital Sources

A cross the range of urban property types, real estate investment strategies must be amassed and categorized by investors according to the financial performance associated with each type. Investment objectives must take into account the degrees of risk associated with each strategy and the expected returns associated with each strategy. Professor Steven Ott of the University of North Carolina at Charlotte has designed a comparison of investment strategies, which appears as table 6.

Austin, Texas, is home to high-tech industries, educational institutions, and government agencies.
GREGOBAGEL/ISTOCK.COM

TABLE 6: INVESTMENT STRATEGIES COMPARED

Investment strategy	Target net IRR*	Income or value expectation	Asset types	Market focus	Portfolio diversification and risk	Debt combination
Core	5–7%	Income	Class A and premium multitenant	Primary markets	Well diversified Low risk	Low: <30%
Core-plus	7–10%	Income and some value creation	Core-type assets with vacancies or repositioning potential	Primary or secondary locations	Diversified Moderate risk	Moderate: <55%
Value-add	10–14%	Value creation with some income	Class A and B with high vacancies Rents below market Obsolete properties with repositioning potential	Recovery primary or secondary and tertiary markets	Moderate to high risk	High: up to 70%
Opportunistic	>14%	Value creation	Development Conversion Repositioning obsolete Redevelopment	New development or secondary and tertiary markets	High risk Vacant land Distressed companies and properties	High: over 70%
Mezzanine debt	9–15%	Value creation	Distressed loans Gap financing Value-add Repositioning	All markets	Moderate risk Position subordinate to primary lender	High: over 70%

Source: Steven Ott, University of North Carolina at Charlotte.
*Internal rate of return. These are target returns, not what has actually been achieved.

A given urban property type may be evaluated based on such risk factors as its location, age, phase of development, price points, and management characteristics. Multifamily properties, for example, might be considered "core" if they are Class A with a long history of high occupancy and in an area with appreciating rents. Another multifamily property might be classified as an "opportunistic" investment if it is a Class B property that is proposed for substantial renovation in the belief that it will generate higher rents. Such evaluations of risk must align property types with the corresponding investment objectives.

Capital for Urban Real Estate

Real estate accounts for a substantial portion of the nation's wealth. While a significant portion of real estate valuation is attributable to the rapid suburban growth of the last half-century, legacy investments in cities and new metropolitan development make the economics of urban real estate highly important to the nation. The economics of urban real estate is manifested in property values, tax revenues, returns from sales and lease transactions, and wages and income. None of this economic value would be possible without the investment capital to develop, acquire, or improve urban real estate projects. Because of the determinant role of urban investment, it is important to understand the positioning of the types of capital available for urban projects.

The sources of capital for real estate financing must first be divided into debt and equity. Debt financing is suited to particular types of real estate and to specific phases of the development process, such as construction loans or later permanent loans. Lenders of debt financing receive their returns from interest charges and fees, are accorded senior positions for repayment, and are secured by the real estate. As the owners of a project, equity investors typically receive a return drawn from the profitability of the development and expect higher returns because they accept greater risk. A third form of intermediary real estate financing is gap financing, sometimes called mezzanine debt, which can be used to meet costs not covered by either debt or equity and which shares characteristics of both in that it may require both interest repayment and returns from performance.

Table 7 subdivides the debt and equity categories by specific sources of capital, each with its own characteristics and urban property applications.

BANKS AND LENDING INSTITUTIONS

About 40 percent of the total capital available for commercial real estate comes from banks and lending institutions, according to Roulac Global Places, making them the largest financial supporters of the real estate sector. Bank sources typically allocate to construction loans and permanent loans, which constitute the debt component of the capital stack for urban projects. Large money center banks dominate the arena for the largest urban projects in the major metropolitan markets, operating individually or in concert through "club" structures.

Lending for real estate has evolved such that local and regional banks make the bulk of loans for commercial real estate projects in smaller markets. This underscores the importance of personal knowledge of the business capabilities of proposed builders and developers—an aspect of due diligence that has become even more important after the economic turndown. Lending is likely to be focused on customers who have particularly strong local reputations for the capacity to complete real estate projects successfully.

Banks work in a heavily scrutinized regulatory environment and therefore must assess each asset carefully when making real estate loans. The context in which such decisions are made by banks must include their own loss reserves, lending capacity, distressed portfolios, and area employment and demand variables.

COMMERCIAL MORTGAGE–BACKED SECURITIES

The commercial mortgage–backed securities (CMBS) market provides securitization for loans on commercial real estate the way the government-sponsored enterprises have securitized loans in the residential market. Because such lending enhances the leveraging opportunities of capital, the effect is to create lower cap rates and increase property values. As large institutions reenter the CMBS market, they make it possible for projects to be financed on favorable terms that encourage transactions. The CMBS sector is expected to remain a critically important part of the debt capital markets for the foreseeable future.

INSURANCE COMPANIES

Insurance companies are principally lenders but also frequently invest in real estate equity. Insurance companies look for reliable income streams in order to be able to match the actuarial projections associated with their liability structures. Real estate provides a solid invest-

TABLE 7: SOURCES OF CAPITAL FOR U.S. URBAN REAL ESTATE

Debt	Description	2010 U.S. real estate debt holdings (Total: $2,944 billion)	Urban application
Banks, S&Ls, mutual savings banks	Largest sums of capital for U.S. real estate; about 43% of total capital deployed and almost 60% of all debt	$1,735.4 billion	Used for construction loans and permanent loans on the entire range of urban property types
CMBS	Raises capital from public sources by securitizing commercial loans; fully 21% of all capital deployed as debt	$614.6 billion	Focused on income-producing properties with loans suitable for securitization (i.e., office buildings and retail properties)
Life insurance companies	Preferred allocation of insurance capital is to debt, with a ratio of 91% deployed as debt and 9% as equity	$240.1 billion	Typically large "core" urban projects, such as office buildings and commercial centers
Mortgage REITs	Raise capital from public stock issuances and other sources to purchase mortgages and mortgage-backed securities, including those issued by government credit agencies	$184.3 billion	Similar to banks, S&Ls, mutual savings banks, and government credit agencies, but typically use lower leverage
Government credit agencies	Fannie Mae and Freddie Mac provide lowest-cost debt financing for multifamily projects	$150.9 billion	Strong support for multifamily residential transactions
Pension funds	Only 8% of pension real estate investments are in debt vehicles; structured debt, such as mezzanine funds, attracts limited pension allocations	$17.6 billion	Emphasis on core properties through debt funds
Public untraded funds	Some private and unlisted funds are not publicly traded and see limited deployment as debt, only about 6% of such funds	$1.1 billion	Office and retail properties and apartments
Equity	Description	2010 U.S. real estate equity holdings (Total: $1,114.9 billion)	Urban application
Private investors	The third-largest sum of overall real estate investment, and the largest equity source, due to the vast pool of individual investors motivated by inflation and tax calculations	$454.2 billion	Every property type, especially smaller properties less than $5 million
Equity REITs	Raise capital from public stock issuances and other sources to purchase properties. Account for 26% of equity capital	$290.8 billion	Emphasis on core properties with established cash flows (i.e., office building, apartments, industrial, and retail properties)
Pension funds	Provide 16% of equity; use third-party managers to invest in the entire range of real estate properties. Need real estate returns to meet actuarial liabilities	$184.0 billion	Office buildings, apartments, hotels, for-sale residential, industrial, and infrastructure
Foreign investors	Include sovereign funds, foreign institutional investors, and individual investors. Represents about 8.5% of equity investment in U.S. real estate	$95.2 billion	Focused on the gateway cities to which foreign investors can travel easily; office buildings, industrial properties at ports, hotels, and income-producing residential properties
Life insurance companies	Only 9% of insurance real estate investing is in equity positions	$25.1 billion	Large core properties with long-term income streams (i.e., office centers, regional malls)
Private financial institutions	Private equity firms manage funds of capital to achieve specific strategies; hedge funds focus on more opportunistic, higher-risk/return strategies	$46.3 billion	Core funds seek stable rental income from established properties; value-add and opportunistic funds seek upside potential from development or rehabilitation
Public untraded funds	Some private and unlisted funds are not publicly traded and may create partnership structures for tax advantages; 90% are deployed as equity	$19.3 billion	Office and retail properties and apartments

Sources: Jonathan Miller, *Emerging Trends in Real Estate® 2011*, Urban Land Institute and PricewaterhouseCoopers, LLP; Washington, D.C., 2011, page 21; Roulac Global Places, American Council of Life Insurers, *Commercial Mortgage Alert*, Federal Reserve Board, FannieMae.com, IREI, NAREIT, PwC, and Real Capital Analytics.

ment for life insurance companies because the decades-long streams of real estate returns are compatible with the liability horizons of insurance companies. Life insurance companies invested in some of the most recognizable urban office and commercial projects in cities of the last 60 years and as a result are among the major equity holders in America's major cities.

REAL ESTATE INVESTMENT TRUSTS

Real estate investment trusts (REITs) raise capital from public equity and debt offerings as well as other sources, and provide it to the real estate market in two ways: mortgage REITs originate or purchase mortgages and mortgage-backed securities, while equity REITs purchase and manage properties. REITs must have most of their assets in income tied to real estate investment and must distribute at least 90 percent of their taxable income to shareholders annually in the form of dividends.[33]

In 2013, listed REITs raised about $77 billion—$46 billion of equity and $31 billion of debt. Because they must be broadly owned, REITs make it possible for individual purchasers to acquire shares and to thereby participate in ownership of properties or mortgages at a scale and value beyond those that they could acquire individually.

Coming out of the Great Recession, REITs were able to capitalize on improving industry fundamentals to increase both property occupancy and income. Because REITs are required to distribute substantially all of their income to shareholders, this translated into consistent—or even increasing—dividends. REITs such as Boston Properties, an office building firm; Avalon Bay Communities, the nation's second-largest apartment manager; and Vornado Realty Trust, a New York–headquartered office property landlord, all outperformed the broader stock markets following the economic turmoil.[34] In addition to the 200 or so listed REITs, there are several dozen REITs that raise capital through public markets but are not listed on any exchange, along with a large number of private REITs about which information is not available.

GOVERNMENT-SPONSORED ENTERPRISES

Government credit agencies are an important source of capital for multifamily residential projects. In recent years, the government-sponsored enterprises (GSEs)—Fannie Mae and Freddie Mac—sustained the urban apartment sector with development and construction financing. They have been able to provide low-cost debt financing for multifamily projects. GSE debt capital for multifamily projects is funded by bonds, whose proceeds are used to purchase apartment mortgages that are packaged and sold in the global capital markets with the agencies' imprimaturs. Even as the GSEs are restructured following the reversals they suffered during the Great Recession, it is anticipated that the national importance of securitization of single-family loans and the generation of capital for multifamily projects will require the design of a housing finance system that will be a continuing force in urban real estate markets.

PENSION FUNDS

The real estate investments of pension funds are typically equity investments. Major public pension systems participate as equity lenders in the development and acquisition of many kinds of urban real estate. Pension systems are repaid from rents from income properties or from the sales of these assets at the end of a specific period. Many pension systems invest through third-party real estate managers who have expertise in particular property types. Pension systems usually seek to have a broad representation of real estate types in their portfolios. A smaller pension system may select a few managers whom they empower to invest in a broad range of urban property types in order to have balanced access to various types of properties,

Institutions and individuals from around the world invest in U.S. property because of the country's economic and political stability.
KOHN PEDERSEN FOX ASSOCIATES

with emphasis on the most basic and risk-averse core assets.

As pension systems become larger and develop more extensive real estate strategies, they often choose to invest in narrower specializations across the real estate spectrum in order to deepen their positions in higher-risk/return sectors. For example, the largest pension systems may hire dozens of real estate managers with targeted sector specialties, such as hotels in gateway cities, multifamily projects in high-growth markets, or medical office properties.

There are thousands of pension systems across the nation, ranging from the public pension systems of states and local governments to union-sponsored Taft-Hartley funds and corporate retirement plans. Across this range of types of systems, the size of pension entities ranges from large state systems such as the California Public Employees' Retirement System (CalPERS), with more than $260 billion in assets, to small municipal systems of less than $100 million.

In addition to public and corporate pension systems, there are forms of retirement capital or assembled capital that must be invested. The retirement plans of religious orders and churches as well as the endowments of foundations and universities must continually grow in order to make payments, grants, and capital commitments without shrinking their core assets. Real estate investments are regarded as important vehicles to boost returns beyond the more conservative returns of bonds, as hedges against inflation, and as versatile strategies to meet actuarial obligations that frequently require high-single-digit fund growth.

FOREIGN INVESTORS

Since 2000, investors from Europe, Australia, the Middle East, and Asia have increased their exposure to U.S. urban real estate. Because of the relative political stability of American institutions, the nation's growth prospects, and opportunities in the gateway metropolitan areas with which foreign investors are particularly familiar, large sums of institutional and individual investor capital have been applied to all property types. Some capital comes in the form of sovereign funds, the official investments of national governments, such as the government of China or Singapore. Other capital takes the form of money managed by foreign institutional investors, such as the Dutch or German pension systems. Still other capital may be the personal investments of families and individuals from nations such as South Korea and Canada.

It is estimated that up to one-fifth of the total invested capital of the world's wealthiest investors is in real estate, and many of those international investors view the United States as a good place in which to invest compared with other parts of the world.[35] A survey conducted by the Association of Foreign Investors in Real Estate (AFIRE) found that more than by a wide margin, the United States was voted the most stable and secure country for investment, and that more than 90 percent of respondents plan to maintain or increase the size of their U.S. portfolios in 2015.[36]

PRIVATE INVESTORS

Private investors constitute a diverse universe that includes high-net-worth individuals, family firms, private equity funds, hedge funds, private financial institutions, and private untraded funds. These various sources represent the largest sum of capital for equity invested in urban real estate in the United States: $454.2 billion in 2010, or about 40 percent of all equity capital. The scale of this investment is evidence of the vast pool of interested investors across the nation who view real estate as a good place to grow their capital.

Their investments may take many forms, including land contributions by owners, contributions of family and friends, cash investments by high-net-worth individuals, private-equity funds, and hedge funds. Private investments

range from individuals investing for themselves to large private-equity funds managing massive sums of institutional capital. Smaller-scale investors may directly purchase or negotiate positions in individual urban properties or invest through limited partnerships. Larger-scale placements are sponsored by private-equity firms, which aggregate capital from institutional investors for specific fund objectives. Hedge funds tend to focus on higher-leverage opportunities and on shorter-term returns. Hedge funds frequently become involved in real estate only in connection with a larger target investment in an enterprise, from which the real estate assets are removed and positioned separately.

Looking Ahead

The tendencies and preferences of the various sources of capital will change in the short term with assessments of risk associated with the business cycle, with alterations of regulatory guidelines, and with changes in global capital flows; and, over the longer term, with more fundamental shifts in the roles of financial institutions. Technological innovations will make entirely new sources of capital possible. For example, new capital instruments—such as were introduced with the advent of commercial mortgage–backed securities—will create new configurations of capital for office and retail projects. When one looks ahead, the reforms anticipated for restructuring the government-sponsored enterprises to engage more private capital will affect funding for both multifamily rentals and for-sale homes.

Given the scale of the real estate sector within the capital markets and its relative attractiveness as an investment category, it is certain that real estate investment will converge with the design, development, and construction process to spearhead financial innovation, produce successful projects, and generate robust returns.

CHAPTER 5

13 Trends behind America's Urban Paradigm Shift

The term *paradigm shift* has been overused to describe the big changes in many areas of modern life. In fact, a paradigm shift occurs not when individual innovations are adopted, but when multiple breakthroughs converge to change the way that basic functions of society are carried out. A paradigm shift occurred, for example,

Arverne by the Sea in Queens, New York, was largely unscathed by Hurricane Sandy in 2013 because of its innovative dune system and building designs, which were intended to protect the community from strong storms.
ARVERNE BY THE SEA LLC

in transportation when internal combustion inventions combined with mass production methods to make automobiles accessible to the masses. It also occurred in office processes when typewriters and carbon paper duplicates were replaced by computers and copiers. And it occurred in medicine when antibiotics were paired with pharmaceutical distribution to transform often-fatal infections into inconveniences of a few days' duration. The temptation to overuse *paradigm shift* to describe wide-sweeping changes is understandable when so many aspects of life are changing so fast.

However, one area where it is now clear that enough forces of change are converging to accurately constitute a paradigm shift for millions of Americans is the nation's urban life. Individual forces are converging—and creating a new urban reality. Energy prices are putting a premium on core city locations and on public transit. Jobs in advanced industries, which more and more are located in urban areas, match the preference of knowledge workers who want to live there. Demographic changes create markets for mixed-use and mixed-income models of urban development. Institutions such as research universities and medical centers are becoming the knowledge anchors of the new urban economy, spinning off employment, contracts, businesses, residences, and public amenities. New urbanist designs are benefiting from creative financial layering to produce walkable urban villages.

As these individual forces converge, cities are becoming denser, safer, more diverse in incomes and demographics, more educated as measured by the skills of their residents, more dynamic, more interconnected, more social, more environmentally aware, more attractive as 24/7 locales, and more essential to national prosperity. The resulting places are livable, integrated, self-propelling engines of the global economy and in them we can see the outlines of a genuine paradigm shift.

The Trends

The city-building professions—urban planning and design, municipal governance and administration, real estate and development, architecture and construction, capital and finance, and transportation and infrastructure—must take into account the way the following 13 individual trends are converging to create new moments of opportunity for U.S. cities and metropolitan areas:

▶ Building for sustainability;
▶ Embedding technology in urban real estate;
▶ Harnessing advanced industries and anchor institutions;
▶ Modernizing urban infrastructure;
▶ Addressing mixed-income housing positively;
▶ Preparing for demographic trends;
▶ Taking on density;
▶ Making walkability real;
▶ Adding transit-related value;
▶ Incorporating public spaces and amenities;
▶ Encouraging design excellence;
▶ Developing new approaches to financing; and
▶ Cementing public sector partnerships.

The previous chapters sought to identify the most important of these trends in the context of today's nascent urban renaissance; the following paragraphs present them more explicitly.

BUILDING FOR SUSTAINABILITY

The concept of sustainability has several applications in urban development. One application refers to the use of building materials and the incorporation of energy and water conservation systems in order to minimize environmental impacts. Another includes the growing risks from climate change and the importance of creating resilient cities. Still another application refers to the broader economics of whether residents can afford to remain in a property in the long run or whether the combination of direct shelter costs and external costs of energy and transportation make it financially untenable. Used this way, *sustainability* refers to a household's total budget for shelter-related expenses, including the high cost of an inefficient location. These different uses of the concept of sustainability are interrelated in the sense that energy efficiencies and efficient locations closer to employment centers make it possible to reduce the overall cost of shelter while at the same time reducing the environmental impact.

Important contributions have been made by individual builders, by advocacy organizations such as the U.S. Green Building Council, and by nonprofit community builders such as Enterprise that have designed prototype homes and buildings using materials, HVAC systems, water conservation, landscaping, and construction methods that contribute to a building's sustainability. New technologies make it possible to replace traditional building and home systems with solar water heaters, air-source heat pumps, low-flow water fixtures, low-VOC paints and adhesives, high-efficiency HVAC systems, more energy-efficient appliances, and sensors attached to existing appliances so that they can be operated remotely. Urban developers and builders will increasingly incorporate practices and systems that respond to the growing demand for environmental responsibility. The National Center for Healthy Housing, which created a National Healthy Housing Standard as a tool to reconnect housing and public health, wrote, "Carbon monoxide detectors can alert us to life-threatening situations. Modern, efficient ventilation systems can keep us comfortable, control humidity, and provide clear, fresh air. More-resilient homes can handle climate chaos, withstanding storms and wild swings in temperature with proper insulation, air sealing, structural integrity, moisture control, and more."[37]

Cities will also seek to be contributors to environmental solutions. As the starker dimensions of climate change become more widely understood—hotter daily temperatures, longer heat spells, drier conditions in some parts of the nation, and more violent storms, occasionally with accompanying inundations—urban real estate professionals will have to incorporate climate change into their business calculations.[38] Among the practical implications of climate change for the real estate sector are scarcer water allocations in some regions, impacts on construction worker productivity in hot regions, energy costs for more air conditioning, and flooding in coastal areas from rising oceans and more powerful storms. Real estate professionals will have to calculate the risks of climate-related limitations and construction delays, site restrictions, and insurance costs as formal criteria in project economic models.

EMBEDDING TECHNOLOGY IN URBAN REAL ESTATE

The wave of automation within homes and in cities is growing. Home systems currently exist to calibrate landscaping to weather conditions, to monitor energy use, to tighten security, and to communicate with light switches, locks, and other devices in a smart building or home via a remote tablet or a smartphone app.[39] At the city level, computer automation can help first responders arrive faster, assist police in reducing crime, help lessen peak energy loads, and schedule public transit arrival times.

Automation already helps households and smart communities to lower bills, reduce electrical consumption, draw power from distributed renewable sources, save water, increase safety, and enhance efficiency and convenience. The advent of cloud computing has made it possible for 45 million residents to be connected to "the internet of things" in their smart homes and for entire cities to be interconnected. Shopping online will force changes in the role of retail stores, and the expansion of telecommuting (i.e., working from home) will alter the configuration of office workspaces. Real estate professionals will incorporate smart devices in homes and buildings in order to respond to the marketplace and meet users' expectations of modern, fully equipped structures.

Technology is also affecting the way real estate transactions are carried out and the way urban construction is managed. Real estate professionals can use Google Earth to demonstrate every perspective and attribute of a property. They use customer relationships management software to transmit critical transaction information instantly. Social media have created new ways to communicate with customers via blogs, Twitter, YouTube, Facebook, LinkedIn, online community portals, and ratings sites. Such social media are integral tools for real estate professionals to use in completing transactions and also for responding to such ongoing responsibilities as payments and maintenance requests. Applications of technology to urban construction will include more integrated assembly of factory-produced components, advanced materials for sustainability and cost-effectiveness, and even fabrication of precision parts on site using 3-D printing innovations.[40]

HARNESSING ADVANCED INDUSTRIES AND ANCHOR INSTITUTIONS

The advanced industries powering the new American economy apply research and development to computers and communications equipment, aerospace products, medical equipment, and medicines. They employ a workforce skilled in the STEM fields: science, technology, engineering, and math. These industries operate in parallel with another subset of advanced industries—business service providers that also rely on breakthrough innovations and STEM skills. These include specialists in software development, telecommunications, data processing and hosting, management consulting, scientific development, and financial technologies.

Both groups of advanced industries are heavily embedded in metropolitan economies, which is important because the Brookings Institution reports that advanced industries together account for 80 percent of privately funded

research, generate one-third of U.S. exports, provide 7.4 million direct jobs, and make possible 3.8 million support jobs.[41]

In many metropolitan areas, these advanced industries and the institutions that help propel them are visible as anchor institutions, so named because they literally anchor the economic bases of neighborhoods, cities, and even regions. They take the form of research universities, world-class medical centers, corporate headquarters, research and development complexes, and arts and creative institutions. They often are the largest private employers in a city and the largest contractors of business services.

These anchors drive urban real estate transactions as they create demand for housing for students, faculty, medical staffs, and STEM professionals; for retail and commercial businesses; for incubator spaces, business services, offices, and specialized research parks; and for hotels of various price ranges. As technological innovations accelerate and advanced industries become America's "crucial drivers of global competitiveness,"[42] and increase the employment potential of "inclusive regional economies," as described by the urban leadership assembly, CEOs for Cities, urban real estate professionals should be prepared to build the needed facilities, continue the recycling of urban land, and incorporate the building features and spatial designs that advanced industries and anchor institutions will require.

MODERNIZING URBAN INFRASTRUCTURE

It is difficult to imagine how new urban projects can achieve their full regenerative potential or even succeed as individual economic enterprises amid the antiquated, inefficient, demoralizing, and deteriorating urban infrastructure that characterizes so many U.S. cities. In the core areas of many American cities, water lines more than 100 years old pose health risks to residents and visitors alike. Vehicular traffic lurches along rutted roadways and congested arterials. The potential relief from traffic blockages that could be offered by efficient mass transit is blunted by the reality of public transit—obsolete, slow, unkempt, and unsafe. Public facilities whose appearance and deterioration undermine public confidence in urban governance include aged airport terminals, dated rail stations, dingy parking structures, and rusted bridges, tunnels, and underpasses.

Municipal and metropolitan leaders in the United States must make extensive investments in their basic infrastructure if they are to achieve their first-order goals of creating safe living environments and of positioning cities as platforms for economic competiveness. The contrast between the condition of a great deal of America's urban infrastructure and that in many global centers is sobering. Many of our economic competitors have built gleaming new airport arrival terminals, sleek 150-mile-per-hour intercity trains linked to accessible metropolitan light-rail systems, ultra-high-speed broadband networks, and efficient roadways with computerized congestion pricing.

Each U.S. city must identify the infrastructure that will create the conditions to encourage future private investment in new projects and set the stage for the urban renaissance that so many trends suggest is attainable. The aggregation of those urban infrastructure plans into a national framework of metropolitan needs would be the first step in compiling an inventory of essential capital improvements, and it would be the basis for a financial plan of federal, state, metropolitan, and private funding. It should focus on three levels of infrastructure:

▶ The existing infrastructure that needs repair, such as bridges and tunnels;
▶ The replacement and modernization of existing infrastructure with new technologies, such as interactive power grids linked to smart appliances; and

▶ The installation of completely new forms of infrastructure for the future, such as high-speed broadband services through fiber-optic networks.

New forms of hybrid financing for infrastructure also will have to be developed. One promising approach is the use of institutional capital—pension funds and endowments—as equity and mezzanine capital for infrastructure projects from which a stream of revenues can be returned to investors. Global examples of institutional investments tied to streams of infrastructure revenues on a large scale include airports, toll roads, bridges and tunnels, seaports, and water and power distribution systems. In the United States, reluctance to turn over monopoly public functions to private operators has slowed the flow of institutional investment in infrastructure projects. However, the combination of the alarming deterioration of essential infrastructure, the lack of public funds for large-scale projects, and new models of transparency and accountability in institutional investment may yet lead to collaborative financial solutions in American metropolitan areas.

ADDRESSING MIXED-INCOME HOUSING POSITIVELY

A well-functioning city needs a mix of housing types. The increasing cost of urban residential units in many cities has pushed lower-income workers and even middle-income workers to the metropolitan periphery, further overloading transportation infrastructure. In recent years, some cities have had difficulty deploying public safety workers in weather emergencies because they live so far from the urban core. Private developers and public officials must make workforce and affordable housing a priority. An important means of adding workforce and affordable units is cross-subsidization within a project, with a developer either voluntarily or mandatorily including a percentage of such units. It has been demonstrated that distribution

of those units within a project has no negative effect on the marketability or functionality of the community, and the positive effects for a city are important.

New York City has an active program of low- and moderate-income setasides in market-rate buildings, usually 20 percent of the units in a building. The New York City Housing Authority has a ten-year goal of supporting the development or preservation of 200,000 affordable units. The strategy is to encourage more economically diverse communities within New York City. Developers are incentivized to participate in the program by the city's offers of tax concessions, access to special bond financing, and waivers for physical exceptions they seek, such as those related to the overall scale of buildings and height and setback requirements. Manda-

Denver's redeveloped Union Station serves as a critical connection between the metropolitan area's different modes of transportation. In 2016, the station will offer trains to Denver International Airport from downtown, thereby linking regional ground transportation with international air travel. DARKSHARK0159/WIKIMEDIA COMMONS

tory inclusionary zoning has been offset by the city rezoning to allow for greater density.[43]

The broader principle of mixed-income inclusion is consistent with a fundamental and historic role of cities in the United States, which is to be staging areas or venues for the upward mobility of working families and immigrants. American cities have been essential to the convergence of economic opportunities in the physical space of urban land. New urbanist thinkers, such as Christopher Leinberger at George Washington University, champion urban projects designed to advance social equity objectives. Sustaining and encouraging the existence of mixed-income neighborhoods is central to the efficient functioning of the city economy as well as central to ideals of equity and social mobility.

PREPARING FOR DEMOGRAPHIC TRENDS

Over the next 30 years, the population of Americans older than 65 years of age will double and the number of those over 85 will triple. Minority homebuyers are already approaching 50 percent of the market share for home purchases and in many areas account for 100 percent of population growth.[44] Beginning in 2014, minority children represented the majority of the entry-level school cohort across the nation. These are just a few indicators of the pace of the demographic transformation sweeping the United States.

Because demographics drive neighborhood patterns, consumer retailing, community growth, housing choices, income growth, net worth and savings accumulation, and many public policy decisions, it follows that demographics also influence real estate, land use, and building strategies, and the effects will be pronounced.

In the seniors' residential sector alone, the American Seniors Housing Association reports that the demand for appropriate housing for seniors will increase from 18,000 units per year in 2015 to 82,000 per year in 2030.[45] Residential builders will have to offer new adaptations along the spectrum of senior apartments, independent living, assisted living, memory care, and skilled nursing facilities. But the greatest need will be for a variety of for-sale and rental properties that can accommodate the 90 percent of aging Americans who say they want to "age in place"—that is, live independently in a traditional residence. There will be an immense need to retrofit existing homes, rethink community amenities, build new "life-span homes," and plan innovative variations of entire age-appropriate communities.

In addition, the rapid growth of minority populations means that residential builders must consider affordability, floor plans, locations, and community amenities in order to be responsive to such factors as larger family sizes, multigenerational families, younger average ages, and specific cultural preferences. Experiences in communities with large clusters of minority buyers reflect good sales for homes with more bedrooms, open floor plans for social events with extended families, outdoor play areas for children from toddlers through teenagers, and privacy arrangements for live-in grandparents. Demographic considerations also apply to various types of specialty stores, family-priced hospitality lodging, and the location of new schools.

TAKING ON DENSITY

Stronger demand for core urban sites almost always means higher land prices. Despite some limits on high prices, such as competitive rents or comparable sales prices, increased density is often the only business solution. A 2013 study of the nation's 150 largest cities conducted by the Washington, D.C.–based International Downtown Association used 2010 census data and 2011 local Business Employment Dynamic data to examine population density and job density in central cities and their relationships to urban vitality and opportunity. The study concluded the following: "On average, the population of the ten largest cities grew by 17.2 percent between 2000 and 2010, while the population of the country as a whole grew by just 10 percent in that period." During that time, the economies of the nation's 150 largest cities came to account for 30 percent of all jobs nationally. The study noted the positive interaction between population and job densities per acre as the economy improves.[46]

However, density frequently generates immediate negative reactions from nearby residents and public officials who oppose large structures and increased traffic. The antidote to density is good design and workable responses to neighborhood and governmental objections. Creative designs by architects can break up the massing of large structures, altering heights and varying elevations and exteriors, as well as reducing the unsightly imposition of parking structures. Careful attention to density can generate positive urban dynamics, including a more vibrant neighborhood life and cost-effectiveness in providing public services.

MAKING WALKABILITY REAL

Extensive surveys show that residents place a higher value on urban residential sites within walking distance of stores, public spaces, and employment. Ease of access, avoidance of traffic and the hassles of parking, and seamless integration into the neighborhood streetscape all contribute to a comfortable urban lifestyle. Developers and planners must imagine designs for sites that can be assembled into a compatible pattern of mixed uses to create an urban village. Large-scale projects can be made more compatible with the village scale by varying architectural styles and effectively dividing projects into smaller components.

"Villages within the city" create a sense of identity for submarkets within an urban area, encourage resident involvement at a human scale, and create loyalties to neighborhood businesses. Walkability also entails responsibilities on the part of public officials. Form-based coding is more likely to allow for a compatible progression of village-type uses than traditional zoning, and calibration of the flow and speed of traffic on nearby arterial and neighborhood streets is imperative.

ADDING TRANSIT-RELATED VALUE

As urban cores become denser, public transportation systems can reduce traffic congestion and automobile pollution, enhancing the neighborhood environment. A light-rail system that carries 120 passengers along a city

arterial street removes 60 cars containing two passengers each from the city streets. Mass transit stops are obvious locations for urban residential, commercial, and office projects. As energy prices continue rising and as mass transit lines become more interconnected, more residents will discover the economic advantages and convenience of mass transit. Already, many millennials prefer mass transit–oriented lifestyles. Developers and real estate professionals should probe beyond the obvious sites to explore the potential of underused properties along transit lines to unlock the value of transit-related real estate.

Studies show that the cost differences between a location-efficient neighborhood that is close to public transit, jobs, and community amenities and a driving-dependent sprawl location are substantial. The Center for Neighborhood Technology reports that between 2000 and 2009, transportation costs rose $1,400 for location-efficient neighborhoods while they rose $3,900 for the most driving-dependent neighborhoods. The center conducted an analysis of the impact of transportation-related costs for groupings of communities and found that in the most transportation location-efficient neighborhoods, the combined costs of transportation amounted to 33 to 51 percent of the area median income, while for the most inefficient neighborhoods they added up to 50 to 75 percent of household income.[47]

INCORPORATING PUBLIC SPACES AND AMENITIES

Cities succeed as places where people work, live, learn, and trade. Throughout history, cities have been places where people gather. It is the social nature of people to assemble in cities to worship, celebrate, participate in governance, enjoy the outdoors, exercise, or simply watch other people. James Rouse, the renowned city builder, once said that he designed Baltimore's iconic Inner Harbor principally as a venue for people watching. He understood the importance

The dense village-style development of Birkdale
Village provides amenities to the fast-growing
town of Huntersville, North Carolina, without
disturbing wetlands or sacrificing open space in
this once-rural community.
PAPPAS PROPERTIES LLC

of creating spaces where people can safely relax
and enjoy the urban setting.

Rouse's philosophy of place making was
based on experience and sound reasoning. As
cities become denser and as increased land and
building costs force residential floor plans to be
smaller, social activities are pushed to common spaces. John Naisbett commented on the
people side of technology, predicting that "high
tech" would engender a need for "high touch," a
human appetite for interaction and engagement
for conversation and participation, for places to
see and be seen. This basic human appetite requires inviting physical spaces, places conducive
to social and communal interaction.

Within a commercial project, such space
may take the form of a sitting area with a foun-

tain near retail shops; in a multifamily community, it may be an interior courtyard bordered
by residences. Urban office and residential
properties offer communal tables for lunch or
coffee time, convenient nooks for group internet
use, and well-accessorized gathering spaces for
after-hours socializing.

In its more public iteration, common
space may mean wider sidewalks with shade
trees on a commercial street or a lighted bus
stop shelter for transit passengers. Plantings,
water features, street furniture, public art,
green open spaces, exercise equipment, kiosks,
performance stages, jogging parks, children's
play equipment, plazas, walkways, tables, and
pet parks are all desirable features of the urban
streetscape that help make it more humane and
vibrant. Urban developers should plan them
with forethought in order to generate the vitality that derives from steady flows of activity and
to enhance the safety that comes from having
"eyes on the street."

ENCOURAGING DESIGN EXCELLENCE

A study tour through Frank Lloyd Wright's masterpieces of design reveals that while they demonstrate stunning creativity, pioneering technique, and evocative beauty, many have serious functional flaws that cause them to leak or crack. The curving roof lines and cantilevered structures were literally ahead of their time. Wright's designs outpaced the capabilities of the building materials available at the time.

Today's innovations in building materials and construction technologies, however, have caught up with the imaginations of pioneering designers like Wright. They make possible the gleaming sweep of Frank Gehry's Disney Center in Los Angeles and the ethereal facades of Rem Koolhaas's central public library in Seattle, just two examples of transformative urban designs. Urban spaces are uplifted by the awe-inspiring effects and the sheer architectural audacity of urban design that suggests the limitless potential of the human spirit and which evokes a sense of reflection and appreciation.

Good design is a worthy goal for private developers and public city builders alike. It should be the goal for all kinds of buildings: residential, commercial, and public. Good design helps mitigate concerns about density and improves the streetscape for pedestrians. Today, architects and urban designers can use materials of various textures, weights, and colors; light patterns; nontraditional shapes and soaring lines; water features and foliage; and nearby topographical features to make projects attractive, functional, and economically feasible. Urban developers should make a special effort to bring good design to projects at all price ranges.

DEVELOPING NEW APPROACHES TO FINANCING

Real estate investments have been a significant sector within financial markets. From individual investors to global sovereign funds, investors across the spectrum of capital are part of the process of assembling capital in order to deploy it in real estate projects that generate strong returns. It is not unusual for institutional portfolios to have 10 to 15 percent of their assets deployed in various forms of real estate investments. Great private fortunes have been amassed in real estate finance.

The history of real estate investing has been a continuous progression of evolving instruments, increasingly sophisticated strategies, and broader participation by investors at all levels. The last several decades have produced financial innovations such as real estate investment trusts, which enable individual investors to participate in large projects that would otherwise be beyond their reach, and mortgage-backed securities, which generate capital for commercial projects using the same basic tools that the government-sponsored enterprises have used to securitize mortgages on private residences.

Real estate investing will continue to be a major target for capital allocations for a variety of reasons. Real estate has the commonsense attraction of being tangible and visible. The basic factors that increase its value such as employment growth can be documented and acted upon. The economic performance of various property types is well understood in the context of business cycles and of demographic factors. In secure countries with stable governments and enforceable rule of law, it is a relatively safe and reliable way to preserve and grow capital. Real estate can be an inflation hedge and can be collateralized for lending purposes. Computerized technologies make it possible to create financial instruments to match investors' specific preferences for the size of the investments, tax treatment, risk profiles, geographic concentration, return goals, and property types. For all these reasons, real estate investing will be a mainstay of national and local economies and will grow in volume and sophistication.

The angled glass facade of the Seattle Central Library by Rem Koolhaas lets in abundant natural light and creates an enchanting environment for library patrons.
MOODY75/WIKIMEDIA COMMONS

Looking ahead, it is possible to anticipate some likely developments in capital flows to real estate. For example, the flow of global capital to U.S. metropolitan markets will accelerate since foreign investors value the relative stability of U.S. markets and are particularly attracted to the U.S. gateway cities with which they are most familiar. Institutional investors with actuarial obligations for pension and retirement funds will continue to be attracted to the higher returns associated with various forms of real estate as they seek to achieve returns in the 7 percent range at a time when bond and equity returns average below that target. Investors' preferences will, over the long run, alternate between the acquisitions of stabilized properties and the construction of new developments.

At the end of the cycle of bargain prices for acquisitions related to the recession and the reassertion of strong demand due to population and employment growth, investors will be attracted to the returns from new construction, albeit with precautions for entitlement and construction risks. Some investors—institutional funds, family offices, and high-net-worth individuals—may seek to bypass capital allocators and instead make direct investments in

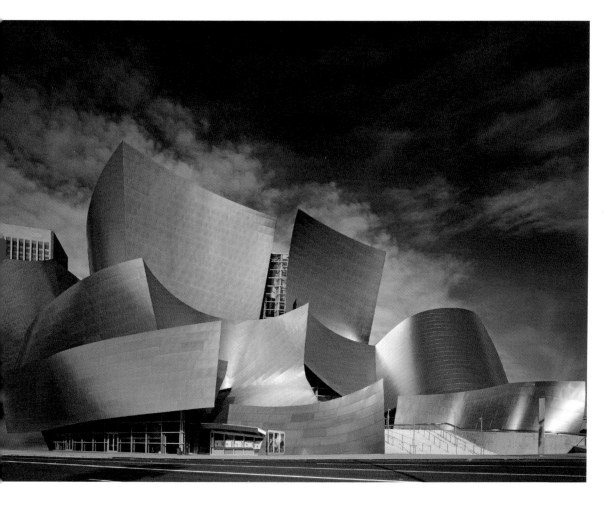

properties. For those investors, relationships with highly competent real estate operators who manage strong pipelines of attractive projects and who have stellar records of performance will be especially valuable.

The Walt Disney Concert Hall, a signature work by architect Frank Gehry, pays tribute to Walt Disney's devotion to the arts and is home to the Los Angeles Philharmonic.
CAROL HIGHSMITH

CEMENTING PUBLIC SECTOR PARTNERSHIPS

Since the 1970s, city governments have taken on a more explicit role in economic development. Prior to that, city governments were widely regarded as responsible only for the essential public safety functions and basic municipal services. But out of the urban tumult of the 1960s it became clear that the nation's cities must become the action end of the federal/

state/local intergovernmental system. Cities and urban neighborhoods were the logical places to address the social issues raised by the civil rights movement: unemployment, income inequality, educational equity, fair housing, and access to health care. This redefinition of federalism put cities squarely in the position of needing to grow their job bases and of becoming active developers of industrial projects, housing and neighborhood retail projects, and downtown office and commercial centers.

Along the waterfront in southeast Washington, D.C., the Yards development includes residential and retail space in a combination of new construction and adaptive use, surrounded by public open space and views of the Anacostia River. Forest City redeveloped the Washington Navy Yard through partnering with the District of Columbia and the U.S. General Services Administration.
FOREST CITY

Over the intervening decades, city governments across the nation have become very capable economic developers, using every municipal resource to attract industries, create advantages, and leverage their assets, services, and capital. For example, cities aggressively enhance their airports to increase the number of direct flights in order to attract industries that require air connections. They expand convention facilities and intensify conference recruitment in order to support CBD hotels and restaurants. Cities build and improve sports stadiums and attract major league teams to increase the range of entertainment options supported by major employers. They invest in industrial attraction and tax retention with financial packages that include payments in lieu of taxes, tax abatements or credits, new markets tax credits, tenant improvement loans, stipends, facilities leases, capital equipment allocations, and infrastructure construction. In many transactions, city governments are the most decisive financial determinant in the job creation and urban development equation.

These economic development calculations almost always involve urban real estate decisions. Cities provide property tax abatements and zoning variances to make the economics of industrial sites more palatable for relocations or expansions. They offer cash outlays from bond programs or tax increment financing to offset the construction costs of CBD apartments, and often they add further incentives for including percentages of workforce or affordable units. Public authorities commit to investing in physical infrastructure to support employment-generating projects, including approach roads, freeway exit ramps, transit stations, easements and rights-of-way, water expansions and pumping stations, electrical power generators, land acquisition and assembly, and leases of public land or facilities. This kind of aggressive involvement by the public sector in real estate transactions is likely to increase as cities become more determined to be masters of their economic destinies and as they succeed in using their powers and assets to connect permanent jobs with the urban workforce.

Foresighted real estate professionals understand the importance of tying into jobs as an economic priority. They can do so by using real estate to situate first-tier job-producing firms. They can develop important supportive projects—such as residential units for the workforce and business spaces for second- and third-tier suppliers that help capture employment growth for urban development. In addition, real estate projects are themselves substantial contributors of construction jobs.

CHAPTER 6

Case Studies

Across the country, developers are profiting from opportunities while helping rejuvenate communities. Among many
projects exemplifying the strategies and trends described in this
book, four are presented in this chapter, one from each category of
city described in chapter 3. Each of these case studies offers lessons

Loft apartments along Cherry Creek in Riverfront Park.
EAST WEST PARTNERS

for those looking to capitalize on the development and investment potential to be found in every American city.

"Consensus strongest" is represented by Riverfront Park, a large master-planned, mixed-use development in downtown Denver. Denver has been thriving in recent years, and this project has made its downtown an even more active and urban place to live and work.

The second category, "mixed rankings with strong measures," is illustrated by a luxury apartment complex in midtown Baltimore, developed by a public/private partnership. Built on the brownfield site of a surface parking lot, it fills a gaping hole in the streetscape and brings more residents to a historic neighborhood.

Next, "mixed rankings with weak measures" is represented by Chicago and Sullivan Center, a conversion of a historic, architecturally significant downtown department store to a modern retail and office complex. The buildings were carefully restored to their original glory while being updated to accommodate today's uses.

Finally, serving as evidence that even the "consensus weakest" cities offer great poten-

Riverfront Park at night, with Park Place Lofts on the right, the Glass House on the left, and Commons Park in the foreground. The park offers an attractive amenity adjacent to the project.
EAST WEST PARTNERS

tial, Detroit's Campus Martius is featured. This urban park—with much support from the local business community—helped spur the current revitalization of Detroit's long decaying downtown. Today, Campus Martius serves as a model for other cities around the world looking to inject new life into their urban core.

RIVERFRONT PARK
Denver, Colorado

Riverfront Park is the result of a 25-year collaboration to create a viable and vibrant urban residential community in downtown Denver. Built under a form-based zoning code, the development encompasses 1,859 privately developed, for-sale, for-rent, and affordable homes. The first units were completed in 2001 and new buildings continued to come on the market as of this writing. The neighborhood fits within the city's grid and is connected to surrounding areas by four pedestrian bridges that cross railroad tracks, an interstate highway, and a river, each funded through a combination of public and private investment. Built on a brownfield and former rail yard, the project was an early model of sustainability. Today, residents can play, wander, skate, swim, and walk their dogs along dedicated nonvehicular pathways or in the community's four parks, paid for by the state, the city, the developer, donors, and residents.

The Site

Denver was founded at the confluence of the South Platte River and Cherry Creek. Over the course of the city's history, the waterfront has had its ups and downs. The Riverfront Park community and the adjacent Commons Park are located at the confluence of these two rivers, at the city's heart. Just prior to redevelopment, the site was owned for many years by the Burlington Northern Railroad and included a huge rail yard and old warehouses. The site offers immediate access to nearby freeway interchanges, and a recently added pedestrian bridge connects Riverfront Park with neighborhoods to the north.

The Idea and the Development Team

The city of Denver had a vision for redeveloping the railroad yards and adding parkland and new development to the area. Trillium Corporation bought the land from the railroad and worked with the city to plan and entitle the area for redevelopment. East West Partners, a resort developer that ultimately purchased the land, became the master developer for the project. And Crescent Real Estate Equities partnered with East West on development and provided critical equity financing to make the project happen.

The idea for the project began during the 1980s with Mayor Federico Peña, who started a dialogue with the railroads about consolidating their railroad lines into fewer tracks, and redevel-

oping the excess land. In 1991, Trillium Corporation acquired several hundred parcels of land from Burlington Northern Railroad, including the Riverfront Park parcels. At the same time, the city was hoping to start redeveloping the area, following on the success that had been achieved in downtown Denver's LoDo neighborhood.

Trillium brought in Design Workshop to help with a planning and design study, and to create a concept plan and design guidelines for the site. A public process was undertaken to prepare and execute a 21-block infrastructure and development plan. In the mid-1990s, a special district—the Central Platte River Metropolitan District—was established, and thereafter Trillium Corporation sold approximately 25 acres along the South Platte River to the city of Denver for a new park, which was a part of that plan.

In 1996, Harry Frampton and Mark Smith of East West heard the mayor of Denver speak at a ULI event in Denver about plans for the South Platte River area, and they decided to investigate the development potential in the area. In 1999, East West, together with the firm's longtime equity partner, Crescent Real Estate, purchased 22.65 acres of entitled land from Trillium Corporation and began the development process for Riverfront Park.

A major reason they were attracted to the property was the Commons Park. Their vision for the project, while similar to the city's vision, was framed by their experience as resort developers. They had spent much of their careers developing resorts oriented around mountain and ski amenities. Riverfront Park, they believed, could be thought of in a similar fashion, but with the city, the Commons Park, and the Platte River as the amenities. Their objective was to create a quiet urban residential neighborhood with easy access to the park and downtown Denver. Essentially, they considered the project an urban resort.

The Development and Approval Process

One of the first public entities set up to engage in the redevelopment process was the South Platte River Commission. Established in 1995 with a charge to create "partnerships among local, state, and federal agencies, [and] private and nonprofit sectors to plan and fund needed improvements" to the South Platte River Valley, the commission was also charged with arranging funding for the parks, bridges, and other public facilities that were envisioned.

The city eventually arranged a deal with Trillium stipulating that the city would acquire the land next to the river in exchange for making infrastructure improvements, including new roads and bridges and a new park. The city also had to invest considerable funds for brownfield remediation; the railroad land had been contaminated with coal ash over the years.

In 1997, the city government and the County of Denver Planning and Development Office, together with Trillium Corporation and Design Workshop, released a plan and urban design standards and guidelines for the area that was then called the Commons. Guidelines addressed streetscape and landscape design, vehicular circulation, blocks and zone lots, a pedestrian active use requirement, setbacks and build-to requirements, architectural scaling, building materials and fenestration, entries, roofs, parking garages, and signage. The plan included a planned unit development (PUD) ordinance, and provided an entitlement to develop according to the plan, but with considerable flexibility. The PUD ordinance was very flexible in terms of a mix of residential and retail uses. It was generally a form-based code, which meant that it generally did not prescribe uses, although it did include deed restrictions that disallowed office space for a number of years, essentially eliminating office uses from the project.

RIVERFRONT PARK LAND USE INFORMATION

USE	ACRES	PERCENTAGE OF SITE
Buildings	14.3	63
Streets, surface parking	5.6	24
Open space	2.2	10
Other	0.6	2
Total	22.7	100

DEVELOPMENT TIMELINE

1991	Trillium Corporation acquires the Riverfront Park site.
1997	Master plan completed. City agrees to form metro district to fund improvements.
1999	East West Partners agrees to purchase 23 acres of land from Trillium.
2000	Design of first buildings begins. Sales begin for first residential buildings.
2001	Riverfront Park Master Association is formed. Three buildings completed. Commons Park opens to public.
2002	Millennium Bridge opens, connecting Riverfront Park to the rest of downtown.
2006	Platte River Bridge and seven more residential buildings completed. Museum of Contemporary Art opens.
2014	Highland Bridge, 18th Street Bridge, dog park, and four more residential components are completed.

DEVELOPMENT COST INFORMATION

Site acquisition	$11 million
Site improvements	$7 million
Soft costs	$91 million
Total development costs	$340 million

PROJECT TEAM

Developer
East West Partners
Denver, Colorado
ewpartners.com

Architects
4240 Architecture
Denver, Colorado
www.4240architecture.com

Oz Architecture
Denver, Colorado
http://ozarch.com

Preston Partnership
Atlanta, Georgia
www.theprestonpartnership.com

Humphries Poli Architects
Denver, Colorado
http://hparch.com

Planner
Design Workshop
Denver, Colorado
http://designworkshop.com

Trillium set aside more than 20 acres for the centerpiece park, swapped land to relocate a public service company transfer station and acquire access to the Cherry Creek bike path, and negotiated other strategic property and tenant deals before selling the land to East West.

Financing

The financing and financial plan for the project amounted to an exercise in phasing and patience. Trillium Corporation acquired the land for an average of around $1.50 per square foot. It subsequently sold land for the park to the city for around $5 per square foot, with the city promising to build the park and provide infrastructure to make the entire project viable. Trillium sold most of the remaining land, 22.65 acres, to East West and Crescent Real Estate for $25 per square foot.

East West Partners and Crescent established a deal in which Crescent put up the equity for the land, and East West managed the development and provided sweat equity. A land loan was also arranged with Bank of America, but most of the land cost was paid for with equity from Crescent, a patient investor. As the development proceeded, profits were split, with 64 percent going to Crescent and 36 percent going to East West

Pedestrian crossings over the South Platte River have created nonvehicular commuting and recreational opportunities for Denver residents.
EAST WEST PARTNERS

Partners. Receiving a preferred return, Crescent got paid first. The financing strategy involved selling some of the parcels to other developers—mostly for apartment development. These early parcels sold for around $45 per square foot, providing working capital to start other buildings in the project. Recently sold parcels have gone for more than $200 per square foot. Each building in the project was financed separately.

East West and Crescent also partnered with Urban Ventures to provide 56 affordable housing units, which are scattered throughout the development and were built by the apartment developers in the project.

Planning, Design, and Phasing

The overall plan and design have been shaped by two infrastructure elements that were critical to making the project work. One was the aforementioned Commons Park. The park and its pedestrian bridge created a highly desirable amenity directly adjacent to the project, greatly enhancing views from the residences and providing active open space for a variety of recreational activities. The second element is Millennium Bridge. This pedestrian bridge over the railroad tracks aligns with downtown's 16th Street pedestrian mall and connects the project to the Union Station area. The bridge, which cost $11 million to build, was partly funded by the developers, who oversaw the design. The bridge has become an iconic landmark. All of the buildings are organized between these two major elements. The plan also includes three smaller parks and a museum.

The plan began with 197 residential condo units in three buildings—Riverfront Tower, Promenade Lofts, and Park Place Lofts—arranged around a plaza and retail area, located between the pedestrian bridge and the Commons Park, creating an immediate sense of place for Riverfront Park. These buildings were completed in 2001–2002, a tough time in the real estate mar-

ket. The ground levels included a coffee shop, a casual restaurant, and Zengo, a fine-dining destination restaurant, adding to the vitality of the initial elements. These establishments remain the core commercial elements for the entire project. There also is a dry cleaner and a dental office. Notes Frampton of East West, "The restaurants were very important for creating a sense of place in this emerging location, especially the destination restaurant."

Traditional Denver materials—including brick, granite, and sandstone—were used on the buildings, but in a modern design. Special foundation layering techniques were used to mitigate noise and vibration from the nearby trains. One of the buildings offers an entrance directly from the upper level of Millennium Bridge.

In 2006, the Museum of Contemporary Art was added to the neighborhood. The museum's land had been sold to Continuum Partners, which used a portion for townhouses and donated the remainder to the museum.

To date, 14 residential projects have been developed in Riverfront Park, with a total of 1,859 units—1,044 rental and 815 for sale. Two additional parcels remaining to be developed will include about 300 residential units.

In addition to the Commons Park, the project includes three other parks—Confluence Park Plaza, the Denver Skatepark, and the Railyard Dog Park. The skate park has become a very popular venue and offers an attractive alternative for skateboarders who might otherwise cause damage to hardscapes in other parks and plazas. The dog park came about as a result of dog owners in the community coming together because they were not allowed to use Commons Park as a dog park. A second bridge spanning the railroad tracks at 18th Street was added in 2010, connecting Riverfront Park directly to the emerging Union Station neighborhood.

Marketing, Leasing, and Management

Riverfront Park has been carefully positioned as a quiet neighborhood adjacent to both open space and the amenities of downtown Denver. The Commons Park has been billed as "Denver's Central Park," and Riverfront Park is marketed to take advantage of this amenity.

When the project got underway, the developers established a sales center across town in the fashionable Larimer Square area, with the idea that visitors to that popular district might be intrigued by what was being developed at Riverfront Park. The center featured a model of Riverfront Park that was updated as new buildings were added. East West also marketed the project to buyers and owners in the firm's resort communities, some of whom wanted to establish urban residences as well. Another critical marketing element was the aforementioned Zengo restaurant, which the developer invested in at the outset to create a new destination that would draw visitors and potential homebuyers to the area. Because of the restaurant, notes Mark Smith of East West, "We were able to achieve rents that we would not have gotten otherwise."

The first phase of residential sales attracted empty nesters, young professionals, and mountain homeowners seeking city addresses. Pricing escalated throughout the first year of sales. Units in the first building—Riverfront Tower—sold for approximately $322 per square foot; larger penthouse units sold for around $385 per square foot. One-bedroom units in the Promenade Lofts—the second building completed—sold for $353 per square foot; the third building, Park Place Lofts, sold for even higher rates, with one-bedroom units selling for $399 per square foot. Affordable units in the first phase were priced in the range of $180,000 to $190,000. By comparison, prices for other new residential projects in the downtown LoDo district were $165 per square foot or less at the time Phase I began at Riverfront Park.

The Park at One Riverfront, completed in 2010, was the one property that was affected by the 2008 financial crisis. Although it took much longer to sell out than the previous projects, it achieved attractive unit pricing. Two-bedroom units ultimately sold for as high as $866,000, or $550 per square foot. Retail space has achieved rents in the range of $28 per square foot.

Management and Associations. The Riverfront Park Master Association and East West Urban Management provide oversight for the whole community, including security, neighborhood cleaning services, landscape services, property management, concierge services, and rental management for condos that are offered for rent. The master association provides governance of the individual homeowner and condo associations.

Community Foundation. A key factor in the ongoing evolution of the neighborhood is the Riverfront Park Community Foundation. The foundation is a nonprofit entity with the goal of incubating arts and education programs throughout the city, and funding projects that improve the lives of downtown residents and workers. All of the foundation's funding comes from the residents of Riverfront Park through a transfer fee assessed on every unit sale in the neighborhood. Currently set at 0.5 percent of the sales price, the assessment generates, on average, more than $300,000 in revenue per year. Funding has been provided to construct the aforementioned dog park, for the preservation of a wetland, and for art installations. Grants have also been used to incubate after-school programs, support art exhibits, fund community health initiatives, and support cultural programming.

Observations and Lessons Learned

More than 2,500 people now live in Riverfront Park. About 10 percent of residents live in affordable units. A wide variety of product is required to achieve a reasonable rate of absorption for such a large project. There are many buyer types, but they all have one or two things in common: they either like urban living and the amenities offered by the city, or they like living next to parks and open space. Or they like both.

One lesson that East West learned early on was that its unit pricing was a bit on the high side. A consultant advised the company that it needed to offer more moderately priced units if it hoped to achieve its financial goals, and this advice led to the Glass House building, one of the most successful buildings in the project.

Essential to a phased, large-scale project like this is a knowledgeable landowner and a financial partner that understand that investing in infrastructure upfront is critically important—and that patience is required, because much of the profits in such a project are achieved at the end, when appreciation reaches its maximum and major infrastructure investment costs are far in the past.

As of 2014, more than $413 million in home sales was achieved, with development costs for these buildings totaling $339.5 million, providing net income of $73.6 million thus far to the development partnership for the for-sale products. Substantial additional revenue has been achieved via the sale of four land parcels, while additional costs have been incurred to build infrastructure, including the bridges and the three parks within the project. Per-square-foot home prices are substantially higher than those in many adjacent neighborhoods, and per-square-foot rental rates and occupancy percentages are in the top 5 percent in the metropolitan area.

Riverfront Park has been especially successful in helping to revitalize Denver's urban core. The addition of pedestrian-oriented infrastructure has been transformative for the city, making it a greener, healthier, and more attractive place to live and visit. The infusion of 2,500 new residents has added life on the streets, boosting the success of downtown retail and entertainment venues.

Riverfront Park has demonstrated the transformative power of public/private collaboration. Success at Riverfront Park involved the cooperation and shared vision of many entities, including the railroad landowners, the city, the land investor, and a creative development partnership that was willing to take the risk to invest in an innovative large-scale redevelopment effort.

THE FITZGERALD
Baltimore, Maryland

The Fitzgerald development at the University of Baltimore Midtown represents a major investment in the midtown Baltimore neighborhood. A transit-oriented, mixed-use project set on approximately 4.6 acres, the Fitzgerald is part of an extensive redevelopment effort led by the university to revitalize midtown.

The Fitzgerald includes 275 luxury rental apartment units, 25,000 square feet of ground-level retail, and a 1,245-space parking garage that serves residents, the university, retailers, and the surrounding community. The Fitzgerald development replaces a surface parking lot; prior site uses included a coal yard and then a Goodyear tire facility. The residential component was the fastest-leasing apartment community in the history of the city of Baltimore, with an average absorption rate of 29 units per month.

The Site

Midtown Baltimore is an eclectic neighborhood of renowned cultural and educational institutions, leafy streets with historic brownstones and mansions, post–World War II apartment buildings, restaurants and specialty stores, and a dense network of transportation lines. Like that of many older urban neighborhoods, its fabric has been disrupted by the urban renewal activities of the mid–20th century that eliminated many old buildings, in many cases replacing them with surface parking lots or vacant lots.

The Fitzgerald, located in midtown Baltimore, reconnects the streetscape and brings life to the neighborhood.
BOZZUTO GROUP

More recent redevelopment efforts—including the Fitzgerald—have sought to fill these gaps to reconnect streetscapes and activity corridors. Bringing more residents to a neighborhood is one way to enliven it in ways that office or retail development does not.

The Fitzgerald is situated on a long, narrow, 4.6-acre site bordered by Jones Falls Expressway to the north, a U.S. Postal Service vehicle maintenance facility to the east, and the Mount Royal

Baltimore Light Rail Station to the south and west. In the surrounding blocks are the Maryland Institute College of Art and the University of Baltimore campuses, the Lyric Opera House, and Baltimore Penn Station, with Amtrak and MARC train service. The development establishes a physical and social link between two campuses. A college bookstore and cafés at the street level draw students and others to what is now a focal point in the neighborhood.

The project was built on a brownfield site. For several decades, it was a surface parking lot. Before that, it was a coal yard and a Goodyear tire retreading facility—activities that caused environmental issues that would need to be resolved before the site could be redeveloped. Despite these significant environmental hurdles, the development team obtained approval for a response action plan from the Maryland Department of the Environment to allow for remediation of the site for residential purposes. The state's Brownfields Revitalization Incentive Program is intended to promote economic development in urban areas and has established criteria and funding for remediation. The developer received $50,000 from the state as well as tax incentives from the city for the brownfield remediation.

Development and Design

The Fitzgerald was inspired by two of Baltimore's most infamous residents—F. Scott Fitzgerald and his wife, Zelda, who, from 1933 to 1935, lived at 1307 Park in Bolton Hill, just two blocks from the Fitzgerald site. Their creativity and their love of Baltimore are what inspired the name of the project and its design themes.

The project began in 2005 with a request for proposals from the University of Baltimore, which owned the land. The university had created a master plan for revitalizing Oliver Street, which runs along the southern edge of the property. In addition to upgrading the area, university leaders wanted more parking for its students and staff. They wanted any new development to be contemporary in design, to coordinate with recent additions to the campus.

The Bozzuto Group responded with a proposal to form a public/private partnership with the university. Ultimately, others joined the partnership: Gould Property Company and J.P. Morgan Asset Management. Bozzuto, which specializes in residential development in the Baltimore/Washington metropolitan region, served as the developer and general contractor.

The project architect was Baltimore-based Design Collective Inc. The firm's design responds

THE FITZGERALD LAND USE INFORMATION

USE	ACRES	PERCENTAGE OF SITE
Buildings	4.0	88
Streets, surface parking	0.1	2
Open space	0.4	10
Total	4.5	100

USES

Retail/restaurant	24,000 sq ft
Open space	77,095 sq ft
Multifamily units	275 units
Total building area	407,712 sq ft

	NUMBER OF UNITS	SQUARE FEET	RENTS (2014)
Studio	30	569	$1,481
1 bedroom	156	730–953	$1,489–1,950
2 bedroom/ 2 bathroom	89	988–1,200	$1,902–2,160
2 bedroom/ 2 bathroom/den	275	1,264–1,411	$2,311–2,661

DEVELOPMENT TIMELINE

2005	University issued RFP.
2007	Site acquired by developer.
2008	Construction started.
2010	Project sales started, construction completed.

DEVELOPMENT COST INFORMATION

Site improvements	$4.5 million
Soft costs	$14.0 million
Hard costs	$56.5 million
Total development costs	$75.0 million
Site acquisition	Ground lease: 3 percent of gross project revenue for 75 years

DEVELOPMENT TEAM

Developer
Bozzuto Development Company
Greenbelt, Maryland
www.bozzuto.com

Architect
Design Collective
Baltimore, Maryland
www.designcollective.com

to the challenges of a long, narrow site by creating two buildings connected by a four-story glass-walled "bridge" at the center. The main entrance—also at the center—is set back from the street, creating a pedestrian plaza. Both build-

Two buildings are connected with a glass-walled bridge.
BOZZUTO GROUP

dryers, and private balconies. Open floor plans are designed around island kitchens with granite countertops and stainless-steel Energy Star–rated appliances. The entire development is smoke free.

Green Features

The development earned LEED Silver certification from the U.S. Green Building Council (USGBC)—the largest residential property in Baltimore City to accomplish this certification to date. Features that helped the building earn LEED Silver include its location on an infill brownfield site, excellent transit access, material selection, energy and water conservation, and construction waste management.

More than 90 percent of the project's construction waste was sent to recycling facilities (versus to landfills) and more than 25 percent of the materials used to build the community were sourced within 500 miles, minimizing the energy required for transportation while also stimulating the local economy. In 2011, the Fitzgerald became the first multifamily community and the first public parking garage in Maryland to have on-site electric car–charging stations. Preferred parking spaces are designated for low-emission vehicles (hybrid and electric).

Low-VOC carpets, paints, coatings, sealants, and adhesives were used throughout. A green roof reduces stormwater runoff while light-colored paving reduces heat absorption. Native plants minimize the need for irrigation.

Financing

The project was financed with $52 million in debt from Bank of America and RBS Citizens, and $23 million in equity funded by a joint venture partnership consisting of the Bozzuto Group, Gould Properties, former Baltimore Raven Michael McCrary, and the New York State Teachers Retirement System (NYSTRS). The 75-year ground lease was awarded through the RFP in 2005 and will generate a long-term stream of income for the university.

ings are configured around private courtyards—one featuring a swimming pool and waterfall, the other an outdoor fireplace.

One building houses the eight-story controlled-access garage, which is designed not to be visible from Oliver Street. The garage is placed at the rear, with six levels of apartments wrapping along the front and with retail space at the ground level. The second building includes four levels of apartments and ground-level retail. With a density of 60 units per acre, the project exemplifies sustainable, urban infill, transit-oriented planning principles.

The parking garage offers rates by the month as well as by the day. It is used by residents, university employees and students, and the general public. The garage is LEED certified and includes two car-charging stations.

Project amenities include an outdoor swimming pool, a fitness center, business facilities, and a media room with theater seating. Units feature nine-foot ceilings, full-sized washers and

Very few development projects of this size secured financing during the economic downturn of 2008–2009; however, financing for the Fitzgerald was closed during one of the most tumultuous weeks in the nation's economic history (September 19, 2008)—a testament to the sound trust and confidence the lenders had in the project.

The economic challenges were also overcome by one of the largest-ever payments-in-lieu-of-taxes from the city of Baltimore, resulting in an abatement of approximately 95 percent of city taxes over 20 years, worth more than $12 million. The project's location within a State of Maryland Enterprise Zone also contributed to the reduction of taxes, providing tax benefits for the retail and parking components. In addition, the State of Maryland Department of Business and Economic Development (DBED) provided the Fitzgerald with a $50,000 grant through the Brownfields Revitalization Incentive Program, and because the site is in a State Enterprise Zone, the commercial components of the project receive a state-sponsored tax credit, which assisted with the retail and garage components. Lastly, the large parking structure, which provides subsidized rates to the University of Baltimore, was privately financed as part of the deal. The project's return on investment is estimated at about 7 percent.

Marketing, Management, and Performance

The residential component was the fastest-leasing apartment community in the history of the city of Baltimore, averaging an absorption pace of 29 units per month and a remarkable closing ratio of 33.2 percent. The community signed an unprecedented 100 leases in the first 90 days of leasing, accounting for 36 percent of its units—even with construction not complete and the staff operating out of a temporary leasing trailer.

The marketing campaign, which is ongoing, includes a printed brochure as well as a strong online presence: a blog, e-mail blasts, social media, and a lively, interactive website that provides rents and other details on available units and allows prospective tenants to submit applications online. Facebook is used to promote goings-on at the property and around the neighborhood.

Observations and Lessons Learned

A unique public/private partnership was formed to finance and develop the property. The project provides the university with a long-term revenue stream (from the ground lease), much-needed parking, and revitalization of a key property in the neighborhood.

The project met pent-up demand for luxury rental apartments in a midtown location. Synergies between the Fitzgerald and its neighboring cultural and educational institutions have added considerably to its appeal.

From an aesthetic standpoint, the building's contemporary design complements the historic buildings as well as the modern architecture that is developing on campus and in the neighborhood, and has helped draw consumers to neighborhood retail and dining establishments.

The reaction from the surrounding community has been overwhelmingly positive. The project has drawn the attention of numerous professional organizations, and has earned several awards:

▶ Winner, ULI Award for Excellence, 2011;
▶ Winner, 2011 Maryland U.S. Green Building Council Wintergreen Awards, Best of Its Kind New Construction;
▶ Winner, 2010 Delta Associates Mid-Atlantic Multifamily Awards, Best Baltimore Apartment Community;
▶ Winner, 2010 Midtown Development Award, Outstanding Development Project in the Midtown Neighborhood;

- Acknowledgment of Contribution to Central Baltimore, Central Baltimore Partnership, 2010; and
- Winner, 2009 Baltimore Business Journal Heavy Hitters Award, Best Financing (project was not yet built).

SULLIVAN CENTER
Chicago, Illinois

Sullivan Center is a complex of nine historic buildings in downtown Chicago that have been renovated and repositioned for modern uses. The first building in Sullivan Center, originally designed by famed architect Louis Sullivan, was completed in 1899 and occupied by the Schlesinger and Mayer department store until 1902, when Carson Pirie Scott and Co. (CPS) bought the building. Other buildings were added over time, and CPS operated a department store in the buildings for more than 100 years.

The original building at the corner of State and Madison streets is one of the most important buildings of early modern architecture and is famous for Sullivan's ornate cast-iron ornamentation that frames the dramatic rotunda entry. Over time, CPS added and acquired more buildings for a total of nine connected buildings to form a 1 million-square-foot complex on nearly an entire city block in the heart of downtown Chicago.

In the ensuing years, many of the historic elements of the building deteriorated, were covered up, or were removed, but the building remained the site of a popular department store, an iconic structure, and a must-see building for students of modern architecture. In 1970, the buildings were designated a national historic landmark.

Joseph Freed and Associates LLC (JFA) purchased the buildings in 2001 and restored them in phases over more than ten years. The redevelopment involved transforming a single 1 million-square-foot department store into a dynamic and modern mixed-use, multitenant project with office, civic, education, and retail uses, including a 650,000-square-foot CPS department store on the lower floors.

The Site and Concept

The redevelopment project grew out of a relationship between CPS and JFA. Notes Larry Freed, president of JFA, "Everything starts with relationships, and our involvement with this project started with our relationship with Carson Pirie Scott, whom we had worked with before. We began the project in a consulting capacity, but this quickly changed."

The buildings were located on a jigsaw puzzle of 20 separately owned pieces of land, including four that were 100-year ground leases set to expire in 2001. CPS brought JFA in to work out a plan to consolidate and renew or acquire the ground leases. The legal and ownership issues were complex, and the city stepped in to help JFA assemble, through condemnation, the various ground lease and ownership interests into one ownership parcel.

The site is bounded by State, Madison, and Monroe streets and Wabash Avenue—essentially the "0-0" point of the city from which all addresses radiate. The site has immediate access to the subway, elevated trains, and major Chicago Transit Authority bus routes. No on-site parking exists, but 4,400 spaces are located within one block and more than 16,000 spaces are within four blocks.

The initial development idea was to restore the building to its former glory while converting and modernizing its upper portions in phases, creating office space above the department store. As the project unfolded, however, CPS left the building and the scope of the conversion grew. The strategy expanded to incorporate more office space and the creation of new multi-level street retail on the lower floors.

Planning and Design

Much of the initial design work was focused on restoration of the many historic elements in the building. Key features of the original design

The keystone building in Sullivan Center housed the Carson Pirie Scott department store for more than a century. It is one of the most important buildings in early modern architecture. The historic structure, designed by famed architect Louis Sullivan, has been restored to its former glory and now houses office and retail uses.

JOSEPH FREED AND ASSOCIATES/GILBERTSON PHOTOGRAPHY

The original rotunda entrance to the department store has been restored and now serves as the main entrance for the new CityTarget store.
JOSEPH FREED AND ASSOCIATES/GILBERTSON PHOTOGRAPHY

included the cornice at the top of the building, cast-iron ornamentation on the first two floors, and the cylindrical main entry rotunda that rounds the corner of State and Madison streets. The developers sought to restore all these features to their original condition using a phased approach.

"Restoration of the building was a bit like an archeological dig, which made the process uncertain, but also exciting," notes Kirsten Hull, development director for JFA. The work often involved surprises, including historic facades that had been covered up for years and secret rooms where original Sullivan drawings were stored.

The various buildings in the project presented a variety of conditions and challenges.

The original terra-cotta cornice had been removed many years earlier, in part because it was deteriorating and pieces were falling off. "A major problem in the restoration of the cornice was that there was no real documentation of the ornamentation, and existing photos showed little detail." The restoration architect was eventually able to develop enough detail to replicate the cornice using glass fiber–reinforced concrete, as use of terra-cotta was impractical.

In the building's interior—especially on the lower floors—are numerous columns with decorative capitals; walls were built around them for protection during construction. The columns were restored on the lower floors, and new plaster casts were made for some of the missing capitals.

The final restoration work, which involved the exterior cast ironwork on the first and second floors, presented a major challenge and required about two and a half years to complete. All the ironwork had to be carefully documented, removed, and sent to a facility where it could be restored.

A principal design objective was to reconfigure and modernize all floors so they would be appealing to both office and retail tenants. The developers sought to integrate the various buildings into one modern space with a large contiguous floor plate. The designers had to work with a variety of floor heights and modify structural walls to create an open floor plate.

A second design objective was to separate and reconfigure the retail and office infrastructure and systems—including electricity, plumbing, risers, fire protection, elevators, washrooms, and HVAC systems.

Because Sullivan Center's large floor plates, high ceilings, and large windows appeal to many modern office tenants, these features were enhanced. The large windows in the building allow for significant daylighting, which further enhances this atmosphere. The reconfigured office space has three lobbies, each with elevator cores.

The retail space is located on the ground level, the second level, and, in some cases, on a lower level. The large storefront windows along both State Street and Wabash are very attractive for retailers and restaurants and have been used very effectively to showcase such tenants.

Financing

A sale/leaseback agreement was negotiated between One South State Street LLC (OSSS), led by JFA, and Sherwin-Williams, which entered the deal because of the historic tax credit opportunity. The historic tax credits amounted to 20 percent of the eligible renovation costs. As renovation expenditures occurred, the tax credits were realized by Sherwin-Williams, which, in turn,

would contribute a percentage of the credits back to JFA to help finance the redevelopment.

The agreement gave Sherwin-Williams, in exchange for its cash investments in the property, a 99.9 percent share in the joint venture before the expiration of the historic tax credits at the end of 2017, whereupon the 99.9 percent owner interest would transfer to OSSS. JFA also contributed equity upfront, as well as considerable sweat equity.

SULLIVAN CENTER LAND USE INFORMATION

USE	ACRES	PERCENTAGE OF SITE
Buildings	2.1	95
Open space	0.2	5
Total	2.3	100

DEVELOPMENT TIMELINE

2001	Site purchased. Construction started.
2006	Phase I completed.
2007	Phase II started. Carson Pirie Scott vacated building.
2011	Target lease signed.
2013	Property refinanced.

DEVELOPMENT COST INFORMATION

Site acquisition	$6 million
Phase I hard costs	$60 million
Phase II hard costs	$145 million
Soft costs	$24 million
Total project costs	$235 million

NET OPERATING INCOME

	2010	2011	2012
Total operating income	$13.6 million	$16.8 million	$20.5 million
Total operating expenses	$7.3 million	$6.9 million	$8.0 million
Net operating income	$6.3 million	$9.9 million	$12.5 million

DEVELOPMENT TEAM

Developer
Joseph Freed and Associates LLC
Chicago, Illinois
www.josephfreed.com

Architects
Harboe Architects
Chicago, Illinois
www.harboearch.com

DePalma Group Architects
Chicago, Illinois
www.depalmagroup.com

JFA was initially turned down for loans by numerous local banks that at that time thought the Loop was in decline and not a wise place to lend money for a historic restoration project. National City Bank made the first acquisition-and-improvement loan totaling $30.5 million. There also was a letter of credit in place for $6.275 million. The project also involved a public/private partnership with the city of Chicago, consummated with a redevelopment agreement that governed about $14 million of tax increment financing (TIF) funds for acquisition of the ground parcels, as well as restoration work. In addition, operating cash flow was used to fund renovation costs. The financing arrangement allowed OSSS to acquire its interest in the property with a minimal equity investment.

In 2007, Carson Pirie Scott vacated its retail space entirely, and JFA began work restoring and modernizing that portion of the building. The developer needed more funds to restore the base building and modernize the newly vacated space. National City Bank indicated that it would need other lenders to participate in the project, so four additional banks joined the consortium. The loan was structured in part to release funds based on the signing of new leases, so JFA immediately began looking for new tenants for the lower office floors and the ground-level retail space.

Despite a difficult economy, the Sullivan Center asset was a growing success, with major retail leases signed in 2011. State Street itself also was evolving and improving, fast becoming a sought-after retail location again.

Marketing, Leasing, and Performance

Sullivan Center uses "19th Century Classic. 21st Century Technology" as its marketing tagline, and that concept was essential to branding the repositioned buildings. "One of the primary leasing challenges for the project was educating the potential tenants on how the building could function as office space," notes Paul Fitzpatrick,

senior vice president with JFA. "One of the early successes in this regard was when we were able to convince the state of Illinois to move into the building and take 250,000 square feet."

Another early tenant helped to brand the new building. The School of the Art Institute of Chicago occupies 160,000 square feet, including a 43,000-square-foot art gallery that is open to the public, and also offers educational programs, drawing many visitors to the building on a regular basis. The repositioning has subsequently attracted stable, long-term office tenants, including the Walgreens E-Commerce department and Gensler Architects. The building's office space is 80 percent occupied with 13 tenants, and office rents are generally in the upper-$20s-per-square-foot range (modified gross).

Target approached the developer with the idea of placing one of its first CityTarget stores in the space. CityTarget opened in the building in July 2012, providing 150 new jobs. The CityTarget store, which includes a supermarket on the second level, was one of three CityTarget stores to open in the country in July 2012. The supermarket is serviced by a special escalator for shopping carts that runs parallel to the escalator for people. The CityTarget also includes a Pret A Manger deli located near the front of the store that is visible from the street. Sullivan Center's retail space is more than 94 percent leased at rents ranging from $40 to $85 per square foot, triple net.

The historic nature of the building and its prime location have served it well in terms of attracting publicity. The restoration work was recognized with American Institute of Architects, Landmarks Illinois, city of Chicago, and ULI Chicago awards, and the project was a finalist in the ULI Global Awards for Excellence competition.

Over the past several years, Sullivan Center has partnered with the Chicago Loop Alliance to support cultural exhibits and programs featuring local artists, students, and nonprofit organizations; for example, vacant spaces have been used for "Pop-Up Art Loop" shows. As a national historic landmark, Sullivan Center is featured in many architecture classes and is a key stop on the famed Chicago Architecture Foundation walking tours.

Sullivan Center, with a strong commitment to sustainability, is one of the few historic buildings to achieve Leadership in Energy and Environmental Design (LEED) for Existing Buildings (Operations and Maintenance) certification and to achieve an Energy Star rating. JFA also worked with several tenants to achieve LEED for Commercial Interiors certification, including Gensler, which achieved Gold status.

The JFA office achieved Chicago's Green Office Challenge Gold level in 2011. The project's carbon footprint is minimized by its location adjacent to major transit lines, 15 bus lines, and newly created bike lanes; the project is also a ten-minute walk from the Metra commuter-rail station.

Observations and Lessons Learned

Sullivan Center's present and future success relies on long-term partnerships and collaborations with the community to craft a shared vision. This dialogue includes the Office of the Mayor, the alderman's office, the Chicago Department of Housing and Economic Development, the Chicago Loop Alliance, the Chicago Central Area Committee, Friends of Downtown, the Illinois Historic Preservation Alliance, and the National Park Service.

One lesson learned is the need to plan and budget for the unexpected. Notes Don James of JFA, "You need to make certain to provide a significant contingency fund in historic restoration projects like this. There are unexpected costs, and time periods often get extended as a result of surprises." For example, there was much more loose and deteriorating masonry than expected.

Kirsten Hull of JFA observes that a typical contingency for a development project is 5 to 10 percent of all hard costs, whereas for an adaptive use project, the typical contingency is 15 to 20 percent. She also recommends that developers

of such projects "budget time and money for ample due diligence and spend money on key professionals to help eliminate unknowns."

From a financial perspective, one key to launching the project was finding a lender willing to structure the loan to accommodate some of the unknowns that crop up in redevelopment projects. Moreover, while there are advantages to working with the same lender on multiple projects as relationships develop and deepen, there can be disadvantages as well; financial problems in one deal may cause the lender to be less flexible on another. On the other hand, working with multiple lenders on one project can be problematic when financial challenges develop because it can be very difficult to get several lenders to agree on a course of action when there are competing interests.

From a broader perspective, urban revitalization is a cumulative endeavor. Establishment of the initial TIF district was a critical first step. Notes Lori Bush, who worked on the project for the city, "The original TIF district that was put in place on State Street was a key element to stimulating investment in the area. You must invest in cities to keep them vibrant."

The concerted effort of the city and JFA to restore and repurpose the landmark Sullivan Center was transformative for the neighborhood, bringing about a remarkable revitalization of State Street, an area that in many ways is the heart and soul of Chicago. Numerous important developments in the area followed:

- ▶ The investment in streetscape improvements and theaters paid dividends and added to neighborhood nightlife.
- ▶ The tremendous success of the city's investment in nearby Millennium Park was instrumental in stimulating tourism that spilled over to State Street.
- ▶ Restoration of the nearby Palmer House Hilton hotel to its former glory was also important, as is the continued expansion of the various neighborhood universities.

▶ The CityTarget is the first retailer to bring a full-selection grocery store to the Loop, which is critical to solidifying the area as a thriving neighborhood in which to both live and work.

These elements and many others have contributed to a reactivated State Street beyond the typical workday, with dynamic retail, entertainment, and services supporting the growing residential population downtown.

CAMPUS MARTIUS PARK
Detroit, Michigan

Open since 2004, Campus Martius Park has become the heart of downtown Detroit's development story and its signature public space. Surrounded by office buildings, residences, and restaurants, it is a magnet for everyday visitors and high-profile events. The goals of the park were to revitalize the center of downtown to be a gathering place as well as a catalyst for economic development, and also to create a positive image for Detroit locally and internationally, year round.

The Site

Located at the intersection of Woodward and Michigan avenues, the 2.5-acre park has transformed the center of downtown from a desolate area to a beautiful and lively oasis in which residents, downtown workers, tourists, and others can gather. At this once-bleak intersection, Campus Martius Park now anchors the city's commercial center. With more than 6.5 million square feet of mixed-use space surrounding it, Campus Martius Park continues to transform its immediate neighborhood.

Development, Planning, and Design

The park is a legacy gift from the Detroit 300 Conservancy, a private, 501(c)3 nonprofit organization created for Detroit's 300th birthday celebration in 2001, and an affiliate of the Downtown Detroit Partnership. The conservancy raised more than $20 million in private funding to design and construct the park and is responsible for management, fundraising, and programming, with an annual budget of $1.5 million. While the parkland is owned by the city of Detroit, the conservancy holds a long-term contract with the city to manage and program the park and all of its infrastructure. The contract was modeled after the Central Park Conservancy, which manages New York City's Central Park.

To develop a vision for the park, Robert Gregory, president of the Detroit 300 Conservancy and an experienced urban development executive, led extensive research on the most successful parks and plazas around the world with the help of the Project for Public Spaces (PPS), a nonprofit organization that advises municipalities on best practices for creating thriving public spaces. PPS worked with the Mayor's Task Force to survey several thousand members of the Detroit community to create a concept and program for Campus Martius Park. With substantial community input, the Mayor's Task Force adopted the plans created by PPS and the conservancy.

One source of inspiration was New York City's Rockefeller Center, a powerfully iconic and much-used urban open space with a relatively small footprint. The conservancy felt that Rockefeller Center demonstrated how a small space can be impactful and helped them convince stakeholders that 2.5 acres could transform downtown Detroit. Through the community engagement process led by PPS, the conservancy came up with a core set of principles the park would need to satisfy:
▶ It should be the heart of the city;
▶ It should connect all major parts of downtown Detroit;
▶ It should serve as an economic catalyst for the city; and
▶ It should attract people year round.

Dan Gilbert relocated Quicken Loans and several other businesses to downtown properties facing Campus Martius Park, including the Qube (center), formerly known as the Chase Tower.
NATHAN WEBER

Through an RFQ and RFP process, six nationally recognized design firms were solicited to submit proposals for the park's design. The conservancy members unanimously selected Rundell Ernstberger Associates, a small firm based in Indiana, to design the park. "We had every rock star in the design world bidding on this," says Gregory. "Nobody had ever heard of this firm, but they showed the most flexibility by taking all these disparate elements, making it uniquely Detroit, and putting their own stamp on it." The design evolved as the firm discussed it with stakeholders, according to Deane Rundell, a firm founder. Above all else, the conservancy stressed that the park needed to be flexible and capable of serving a variety of purposes.

Construction began in May 2003 and was completed in November 2004. An attractive urban oasis is created by the fountains, water walls, monuments, and gardens. The park contains a mix of lawns and hardscapes for active and passive uses, with seating for more than 3,000 people on walls, benches, steps, and movable

Located in the heart of downtown Detroit, Campus Martius Park features a pop-up beach each summer along with grassy areas, concert stages, and an outdoor café.
TOP: DANIEL LOBO; ABOVE: NATHAN WEBER

chairs. It also includes a bistro with indoor and patio seating, two performance stages, and a seasonal ice rink. Currently, an urban beach with sand and beach chairs located adjacent to the Fountain, an outdoor bar/grill, and surrounded by the Detroit skyline draws enthusiastic users. In addition, annual "pop up" features occur, including four outdoor basketball half-courts and a sand volleyball court.

Design and construction of the park cost $20 million, with approximately $500,000 in design costs, $16 million in construction costs, and $3.5 million set aside as an endowment for the park. Compuware Corporation, a business software and services firm, provided $7 million toward its construction, making it the single largest financial supporter of the park's construction.

The remaining $13 million in funding came from several companies and organizations in downtown Detroit, including Ford Motor Company, the Hudson-Webber Foundation, and Bank One. The Kresge Foundation was the single largest donor to the park's endowment. Many of these organizations continue to support the park's operations, but since 2013, Quicken Loans has become the largest annual financial supporter of the park's operations and programming since its construction.

While the Detroit 300 Conservancy focused on developing the public space, the Detroit Economic Growth Corporation (DEGC) supported residential and commercial real estate investment around the park. The DEGC and the city of Detroit coordinated public infrastructure improvements around the park that supported the park's development and enabled sites to be redeveloped from office to residential space. The DEGC was instrumental in integrating multiple street surfaces that intersected at Campus Martius Park, and rerouting Woodward Avenue around the park. In partnership with the Detroit 300 Conservancy, the DEGC and the city helped design the road and raised the state and federal funds necessary to build it and all corresponding utilities.

The conservancy, the DEGC, and other stakeholders supported the development of residential space in downtown Detroit because of a growing demand for downtown apartments, and because adding residents is a key to creating a thriving downtown. Infrastructure improvements spearheaded by the DEGC enabled abandoned "Class C" buildings to be converted into residential space. The DEGC also played a pivotal role in developing the area around the park by acquiring sites and making them available to developers through an RFP process. Some of the major funders of the park, such as Compuware, built corporate headquarters on the sites that were managed by the DEGC.

CAMPUS MARTIUS LAND USE INFORMATION

USE	ACRES	PERCENTAGE OF SITE
Open space: Main park	1.75	70
Open space: Cadillac Square	0.75	30
Total	2.5	100

DEVELOPMENT TIMELINE

1999	Task force created to establish the park.
2000	Design team selected.
2001	Plans presented to the public.
2003	Agreements approved, construction began.
2004	Construction completed, grand opening.

DEVELOPMENT COST INFORMATION

Design	$0.5 million
Construction	$16.0 million
Total project costs	$16.5 million

NET OPERATING INCOME

Annual budget	$1.25 million
Park endowment	$3.5 million

PROJECT TEAM
Developer
Detroit 300 Conservancy with the city of Detroit
Detroit, Michigan
www.detroit300conservancy.com

Architect
Rundell Ernstberger Associates
Indianapolis, Indiana
www.realsite.com

Management and Programming

The park offers more than 250 activity days annually, including several high-profile events such as the Super Bowl XL Festival and the *Today* show. Programming seeks to attract all kinds of people and to make the park a year-round, round-the-clock facility. Programming ranges from morning yoga classes to Friday night beach parties. The park's Classical Tuesday Nights feature ensembles from the Detroit Symphony Orchestra, and the park regularly hosts a 4th Friday night concert featuring the best of Detroit music. Periodic movie nights as well as Saturday afternoon kids' shows and theater performances

Campus Martius Park is a two-square-block district in the commercial center and heart of downtown Detroit.
NATHAN WEBER

provide family-friendly entertainment that draws residents of all ages. A lunchtime music series, a happy-hour concert series, beach parties, a weekly farmers' market, lunchtime food trucks, a "Tech Talk" lecture series, and several health and fitness activities round out the offerings. Another way the conservancy uses entertainment to activate the park is by having local singer-songwriters play in the market spaces, which drives traffic to food trucks and has helped make the vendors a success.

The variety of programming creates a constant sense of activity in the park. Passersby are drawn into the latest activity, and tourists as well as residents know that they can visit spontaneously because something is always going on. Even in the winter, the park continues to draw large crowds.

National events draw substantial positive media attention to the city. When the Super Bowl was held in Detroit in 2006, the park was the headquarters for the official after-party, and major media outlets attended. Covering the Super Bowl, the *Tonight Show* and other international media outlets drew a great deal of media attention showcasing the Campus Martius rink and a weekend of music, a snow slide, and festivities. Although less common, private events like weddings also have created buzz and generated beautiful images of the park that have come to symbolize the city of Detroit.

Impact on Downtown

Robert Gregory estimates that approximately $20 million spent on Campus Martius Park has leveraged $1.6 billion of investment in downtown Detroit since 2003. These transformational investments in the public space were led by the private sector with support from the Economic Growth Corporation and the city.

In 2003, Compuware Corporation completed a $400 million, 16-story headquarters fronting on the park. "The park played a major role in our decision to move to Detroit," says Peter Karmanos Jr., Compuware founder and CEO.

In 2010, Dan Gilbert, CEO of Quicken Loans, the second-largest mortgage company in the United States, made a conscious effort to help Detroit's revitalization by moving its 1,700-employee world headquarters from suburban Livonia to downtown. The Detroit native had seen young graduates turn down his companies' offers to move to remote suburban locations, and believed that the revival of downtown was key not only to the city's success, but also to his own.

Gilbert and his family of companies, all held under Rock Ventures, have made several downtown real estate acquisitions since Campus Martius Park opened, starting with the Madison Theater Building, which he transformed into a tech hub. Later that year, Gilbert bought and renovated the Chase Tower, and moved 2,000 Quicken Loans employees into it. Rock Ventures continued investing in real estate around the park and acquired some of Detroit's most iconic downtown buildings such as the Dime Building and the First National Building. According to Gregory, most of these downtown buildings had been substantially empty before Gilbert's companies moved in. Gilbert now owns more than 40 downtown buildings and his companies have been responsible for moving a total of 12,000

employees into the downtown in under four years. Gilbert's influence has created a downtown tech community, with tenants and other stakeholders referring to Woodward Avenue, which runs around Campus Martius Park, as "Webward Avenue."

In 2005, a new ten-story office building was built on the site of the old Detroit City Hall. The building, known as 1 Kennedy Square, is home to approximately 400 employees of the accounting firm Ernst & Young. The building drew attention in the spring of 2014 when a Starbucks opened in one of the lower-level commercial spaces. The new Starbucks marked a move back into Detroit for the Seattle-based coffee company after it had closed two downtown locations nearly six years earlier.

The historic Book Cadillac Hotel reopened in 2008 after a $200 million renovation. The hotel had been closed for decades, but now operates as the Westin Book Cadillac Hotel. The hotel has been a boon for downtown, hosting convention visitors, tourists, and business and pleasure travelers. The hotel also generates visitors to the park, since patrons ask the concierge what to see and Campus Martius is a natural choice.

GalaxE.Solutions, a New Jersey–based information technology firm, announced in April 2013 that it would spend $4.2 million to rehab 27,000 square feet of a building on the park's northwest corner and create 500 jobs over the next four years. Tim Bryan, GalaxE.Solutions chairman and CEO, explained, "GalaxE.Solutions selected 1001 Woodward Avenue as our Detroit IT development facility because it was perfectly situated next door to Compuware, and soon, Quicken Loans. By locating next to beautiful Campus Martius, we have brought together all the ingredients for a Detroit IT hub to compete with international cities. The park is outstanding and offers the kind of recreation and relaxation that urban professionals prize. It will be a key element in attracting new employees to the downtown. We are thrilled to be here in Detroit

Outdoor seating fills up at Detroit's Campus Martius Park each summer.
NATHAN WEBER

right next to Campus Martius." The company now houses 150 employees in Detroit and has been an outspoken supporter of the city, with its "Love, Detroit" media campaign that encourages people to visit.

In 2012, Blue Cross Blue Shield of Michigan relocated its 3,400-employee headquarters from suburban Southfield, Michigan, to downtown Detroit, bringing its total downtown presence to about 6,400 employees in several buildings. Relocated employees were overwhelmingly positive about the move. Several other major tenants also have relocated to buildings nearby the park, continuing downtown Detroit's rebirth.

Observations and Lessons Learned

Campus Martius Park has exceeded all expectations. It is the most active year-round space in downtown Detroit, providing an outstanding environment for the more than 2 million annual visitors. More than $1 billion in new development has occurred within a two-block radius of the park.

One of the central challenges to making Campus Martius Park a success was developing consistent funding streams to maintain and operate it. Ongoing operations and programming have come primarily from donations from the corporations around the park. A business improvement district started up in 2014 and is expected to help with future operations funding.

Programming, which is considered a critical element of the park's success, has relied on voluntary contributions from this local corporate community. In addition to local corporate donations, various other companies support the park by acting as official sponsors for its programming. Revenues from the businesses in the park itself, such as the ice rink, the Fountain Bistro, and food kiosks, also support Campus Martius's operations. Finally, growth of the park's small endowment also provides it with some additional annual funding.

Campus Martius received national recognition in 2010 when it was chosen as the first-ever recipient of the ULI Amanda Burden Urban Open Space Award. Presenting the award, Burden, who was commissioner of the New York City Department of City Planning at the time, said, "Campus Martius exemplifies the social and economic transformative effect of great public centers of activity, respite, and social interaction." In the same year, the park was ranked as one of the top ten public spaces by the American Planning Association.

Dennis Archer, the former Detroit mayor who started planning for the park, says, "Winning the award made years of work worthwhile. For us to come out number one—that's huge," he says. "I really wanted something that would capture people's imagination. And we got it."

The conservancy is using Campus Martius as a model for a series of other urban parks it is creating throughout downtown Detroit:

▶ Capitol Park is the center of an arts district and residential neighborhood that will become home to approximately 1,000 residents.
▶ Grand Circus Park is a key gateway into downtown, built at the turn of the 1900s but since fallen into disrepair. It is being turned into public space surrounded by a significant residential neighborhood.
▶ Paradise Valley–Beatrice Buck Park will be the focal point of an entertainment district that celebrates the neighborhood's African American history.

Campus Martius Park has become the most active pedestrian area in downtown Detroit. It is widely recognized internationally as one of the best central squares and signature urban public spaces. Given its location in a city that is undergoing unprecedented economic and social change, Campus Martius is worthy of special recognition and emulation.

Conclusion

Many forces are at work that are enhancing the role of metropolitan areas as engines of the new American economy. The key dynamics propelling the American economy—growing population, job-creating innovations in technology and the life sciences, increasing global trading volumes, improvements in higher education and training, sustainability technologies, supportive infrastructure, and communication systems that enrich the productivity of

human interactions—are all gathering strength within the nation's cities. These dynamics are most pronounced within the physical geography of our cities, and each requires physical real estate. The adaptation of older urban real estate to modern purposes and the development of new forms of the built environment in cities ensure that urban real estate investment will be a productive enterprise of long duration.

The volume of capital required to support the scale of both recycled uses and new developments requires resourcefulness in aligning traditional sources of capital for urban projects as well as creativity in applying capital in new ways. Urban real estate investing will continue to be a fertile field for small individual investors as well as for global sovereign funds; for niche debt tactics as well as for massive equity strategies; for the most traditional of "core" positions as well as for

the most aggressive of "opportunistic" appetites; and for downtown megastructure visionaries as well as for walkable-neighborhood urbanists.

Urban real estate investment constitutes a powerful domestic engine that will help determine the shape of the national landscape and which will make possible bright futures for those skillful enough to imagine, invest, and execute wisely. To see beyond the years and envision what the future holds for U.S. cities, developers, planners, policy makers, and investors must understand the trends that are occurring today. Taken together, the individual dynamics discussed in this book are components of an American mosaic that tells an exciting story of a new urban age. This quickly urbanizing world and the postrecession economic order still in the making offer a promising moment of opportunity for all of America's cities.

Notes

1 Brookings Institution Metropolitan Policy Program, "Shaping a New Federal Partnership for a Metropolitan Nation" (Washington, DC: Brookings Institution, 2008), 13.

2 U.S. and World Population Clock, U.S. Census Bureau, www.census.gov/popclock.

3 U.S. Census Bureau, "The Next Four Decades: The Older Population in the United States: 2010 to 2050," May 2010.

4 World Wildlife Fund for Nature, "Reinventing the City: Three Prerequisites for Greening Urban Infrastructure," 2010, www.wwf.se/source.php/1481769/WWF_Low_Carbon_Cities_2012.pdf.

5 Risky Business: The Economic Risks of Climate Change, http://riskybusiness.org, June 2014.

6 City of New York Department of City Planning, "New York City Population Projections by Age/Sex & Borough, 2010–2040" (New York: City of New York Department of City Planning, 2013), 2, www.nyc.gov/html/dcp/pdf/census/projections_report_2010_2040.pdf.

7 Paul R. Levy, founding chief executive of Philadelphia's Center City District (CCD). Levy and Lauren M. Gilchrist wrote Downtown Rebirth: Documenting the Live-Work Dynamic in 21st Century U.S. Cities, prepared for the International Downtown Association by the Philadelphia Center City District, 2013, www.defining-downtown.org.

8 U.S. Census Bureau, "The Next Four Decades."

9 Michael D. McCall, "Deep Drop in Retail Trade Employment during the 2007–09 Recession," Monthly Labor Review, April 2011, 45–48.

10 Deutsche Asset & Wealth Management, U.S. Real Estate Strategic Outlook, February 2014, 11.

11 Krystina Gustafson, "Without rebirth, malls face extinction: Developer," CNBC, Jan. 13, 2014, www.cnbc.com/id/101329283.

12 RREEF Property Trust, "Bricks and Clicks: Rethinking Retail Real Estate in the E-commerce Era," July 2012, 2, http://realestate.deutscheawm.com/content/_media/Research_RREEF_Real_Estate_Bricks_and_Clicks_July2012.pdf.

13 Ohio Development Services Agency Research Office, "Ohio Major Employers–Section 1," April 2014, http://development.ohio.gov/files/research/B2001.pdf.

14 Brie Zeltner, "Cleveland Clinic, CWRU announce plan to build new medical education building on Clinic campus," June 2, 1013, www.cleveland.com/healthfit/index.ssf/2013/06/cleveland_clinic_cwru_announce.html.

15 Timothy Magaw, "Cleveland Clinic, Case Western Reserve University plans for medical education hub expand," Crain's Cleveland Business, November 25, 2014, 1.

16 Francys Vallecillo, "New York Led U.S. Office Market Growth in 2013," World Property Journal, Jan. 23, 2014, www.worldpropertyjournal.com/north-america-commercial-news/us-office-leasing-new-york-san-francisco-cushman-wakefield-commercial-property-2013-maria-sicola-7919.php.

17 CBRE Econometric Advisors Outlook.

18 San Jose Mercury News, 2014.

19 Adele Hayutin, "Changing Demographic Realities," in Independent for Life: Homes and Neighborhoods for an Aging America, ed. Henry Cisneros, Margaret Dyer-Chamberlain, and Jane Hickie (Stanford, CA: Stanford Center on Longevity, 2012), 36.

20 Keith Wardrip, "Strategies to Meet the Housing Needs of Older Adults," Insight on the Issues, No. 38, March 2010.

21 RealtyTrac, www.realtytrac.com/content/foreclosure-market-report/realtytrac-housing-market-recovery-index-7839.

22 U.S. Census Bureau, "The Next Four Decades."

23 National Center for Healthy Housing and the American Public Health Association, National Healthy Housing Standard (Columbia, MD: National Center for Healthy Housing, 2014), www.nchh.org/standard.aspx.

24 U.S. Census Bureau, New Privately Owned Housing Units Started, Annual Data, https://www.census.gov/construction/nrc/pdf/startsan.pdf.

25 U.S. Department of Housing and Urban Development, "America's New Economy and the Challenge of Cities: A HUD Report on Metropolitan Economy Strategy," 1996.

26 Urban Land Institute and Pricewaterhouse Coopers, Emerging Trends in Real Estate® 2011 (Washington, DC: Urban Land Institute and Pricewaterhouse Coopers LLP, 2010), 47.

27 Paul Merrion, "Emanuel's infrastructure trust looks to help commercial landlords," Crain's Chicago Business, Aug. 2, 2014, www.chicagobusiness.com/article/20140802/ISSUE01/308029972/emanuels-infrastructure-trust-looks-to-help-commercial-landlords.

28 "Expansion of Fiber Networks Helps Drive Development," Community Development Digest, July 24, 2013, 1.

29 Urban Land Institute and Ernst & Young, Infrastructure 2010 (Washington, DC: Urban Land Institute and Ernst & Young, 2010), 5.

30 PwC and the Urban Land Institute, Emerging Trends in Real Estate® 2014 (Washington, DC: PwC and the Urban Land Institute, 2013).

31 Baltimore Development Corporation, http://baltimoredevelopment.com/projects-and-programs/neighbourhood-development/.

32 Bureau of Labor Statistics, U.S. Department of Labor.

33 Charles Long, *Finance for Real Estate Development* (Washington, DC: Urban Land Institute, 2011), 107.

34 A.D. Pruitt, "Bragging Rights for REITs," *Wall Street Journal*, July 13, 2011, C-10.

35 Francys Vallecillo, "World's Ultra Wealthy Hold $5.3 Trillion in Real Estate," *World Property Journal*, Jan. 15, 2014, www.worldpropertyjournal.com/europe-residential-news/ultra-wealthy-individuals-savills-wealth-x-global-real-estate-investment-7886.php.

36 Association of Foreign Investors in Real Estate, "Annual Foreign Investment Survey 2015."

37 National Center for Healthy Housing, 1.

38 *Risky Business.*

39 Sam Frizell, "This Startup is Trying to Create—and Control—the Internet of Your Home," *Time*, June 26, 2014, http://time.com/2926400/at-your-service.

40 Ron Nyren, "Technology Outlook," *Urban Land*, November/December 2012, 44–47.

41 Mark Muro, Kenan Fikri, and Scott Andes, "Powering Advanced Industries: State by State," Brookings Advanced Industries Series (Washington, DC: Brookings Institution, 2014), 3, www.brookings.edu/~/media/research/files/papers/2014/02/19-ai/advancedindustriesstatebystate.pdf.

42 Ibid.

43 Julie Satow, "Living in the Mix," *New York Times*, August 29, 2014, www.nytimes.com/2014/08/31/realestate/affordable-housing-in-new-yorks-luxury-buildings.html.

44 Patrick Lynch and Leonard Bogorad, "Demographic Trends Support Robust Multifamily Demand," *The Advisory*, August 8, 2013, www.rclco.com/advisory-demographic-trends-support-robust-multifamily-demand.

45 Noah N. Weiss and Debra A. Cafaro, "Senior Housing: Core Assets with Above-Core Returns." *PREA Quarterly*, Summer 2013, 53.

46 Paul R. Levy, International Downtown Association, "Downtown Areas Are Growing," *Community Development Digest*, October 2013, 1.

47 "Living in Sprawl Costs Thousands Extra per Year," *Better Cities and Towns*, April/May 2012, 9.